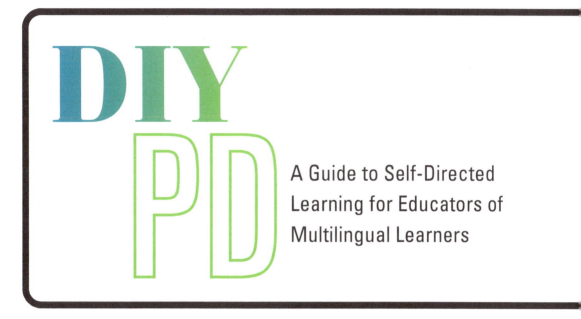

DIY PD

A Guide to Self-Directed Learning for Educators of Multilingual Learners

By Katie Toppel, Tan Huynh, and Carol Salva

Published by Seidlitz Education
P.O. Box 166827
Irving, TX 75016
www.seidlitzeducation.com

Copyright © 2021 Seidlitz Education

No part of this book may be reproduced in any form or by electronic or mechanical means, including photocopy, recording, scanning, or other, without prior permission from the publisher.

To obtain permission to use material from this work, please submit a written request to Seidlitz Education Permissions Department, P.O. Box 166827, Irving, TX 75016

For related titles and support materials visit www.seidlitzeducation.com.

9.21

contents

Acknowledgments. 5

Foreword by Larry Ferlazzo & Katie Hull-Sypnieski 6

Chapter 1: Getting Started with Self-Directed Learning 8

Chapter 2: INTERPRETIVE Professional Learning 16

Chapter 3: EXPRESSIVE Professional Learning 42

Chapter 4: INTERACTIVE Professional Learning 66

Chapter 5: EXTENDING Professional Learning. 94

About the Authors. 111

Bibliography 112

ACKNOWLEDGMENTS

To my greatest loves: John, Grace, and Sammy.
— Katie

To the two ladies who have sacrificed more than I can repay in 100 lifetimes: Mom and Che Nhu.
— Tan

To my incredible family: Brad, Anthony, Nicholas, and Angelica. You are my greatest teachers. You have my love and gratitude.
— Carol

We would like to thank the following bloggers and educators in the field for their contributions to this work: Laura Baker, Jess Bell, Aimee Biggs, Dorina Ebuwa, Alexa Epitropoulos, Sheri LeDrew, Larry Ferlazzo, Justin Garcia, Jennifer Gonzalez, Valentina Gonzalez, Jennifer Hunter Dillon, Michelle Makus Shory, Irina McGrath, Maria Montroni-Currais, and Colleen Thompson. We would also like to thank Andrea Honigsfeld, Nancy Motley, Derek Rhodenizer, Rhonda Gadino and Katie Hull-Sypnieski for their time and insight.

Foreword

Although teachers can learn much from high-quality, well-delivered staff development, it is never fun to have to sit through "canned" presentations from representatives of textbook companies or a workshop that isn't a match for one's current role. Sometimes secondary teachers have to attend workshops led by people who have only taught in elementary school, or elementary teachers have to attend sessions led by those who have only secondary experience.

This challenge of mismatched staff development can be particularly problematic for teachers of English learners. For example, in some districts there are few teachers of ELs and–with money tight–professional development for teaching ELs is sometimes not a priority.

So, given this state of affairs, what are teachers of ELs and other EL advocates (coaches and administrators) supposed to do?

As a first step, we would suggest reading this book or–even better–getting other teachers in your district to read it with you!

Katie Toppel, Tan Huynh, and Carol Salva have written a step-by-step guide for teachers of ELs to get the professional development they need and want. We're particularly impressed–and we think you will be, too–about how they have divided these PD experiences into three practical categories: interpretative, expressive, and interactive. Looking at professional development through those three lenses has changed our perspectives about all PD.

They present strategies, research, and their own experiences revealing how they have applied those same techniques and research results in their own work. They also give clear suggestions as to how teachers, coaches, and administrators can do the same, as well as providing a cornucopia of additional resources.

We have learned through our experience that good teaching for ELs is usually good teaching for all students. In the same vein, good professional development for educators of ELs tends to be good professional development for all educators. The reflective practices, research-based strategies, and anecdotal classroom experiences described in this book can be a model for all educators seeking professional development in nearly any aspect of schooling.

Not only does this book serve as a guide for professional development, it also provides the connections needed to help us as teachers develop a sense of collegiality with other teachers of ELs around the world. It offers advice and encouragement about how we can share our experiences with others and–believe us–you can't put a price on the energy that can be gained from that kind of intellectual stimulation.

The number of English learners in our schools is only going to be increasing in the future, and educators will clearly need more support with these rising numbers. *DIY PD: A Guide To Self-Directed Learning Of Multilingual Learners* is an essential playbook for how educators can hone their skills to benefit their students.

The wisdom we have gained from Katie, Tan, and Carol over the years has improved our teaching practices. We're thrilled and honored that they invited us to write this foreword and excited that more of our sister and brother advocates and teachers of ELs can now learn from their experiences as well.

–Larry Ferlazzo &
Katie Hull-Sypnieski

1

GETTING STARTED
with SELF-DIRECTED LEARNING

Back in the summer of 2019, we all met in Dallas to plan this book you're now holding. Carol had booked professional learning engagements all the way to the next summer. Katie and Tan were still going to their schools and teaching. Our lives flowed on as usual.

Then the world turned upside down, not just for the three of us, but for everyone.

Tan
On a Sunday evening in early February, an email notification entitled "School Closure" popped up on my phone. It explained that all schools in Ho Chi Minh City, Vietnam, were closing by government mandate, and that on Monday, we teachers would report to school as usual to prepare for virtual schooling – something most of us had zero experience with. Little did my colleagues and I realize that the past Friday was to be the last day we would be physically at school with our students for a long time. What was supposed to be just a two-week holding pattern turned into an experience that stretched into months.

For the first six weeks, my colleagues and I still met in person at school, collaborated, and facilitated virtual learning. Then the rug was abruptly pulled out from under us again when another Sunday night email notified teachers that on the upcoming Tuesday, educators must work from home to further enforce physical distancing measures. The last thread of face-to-face human interaction on campus was severed. We had already lost our in-person connection with our students and now we were losing our in-person connection with our colleagues as well. Our hearts could not take any more bruising.

As the world was crumbling in Asia, Carol and Katie started experiencing the first warning signs of the coming storm in the United States. Carol had been invited to be the keynote speaker at the Confederation of Oregon School Administrators 2020 State English Learners Alliance Conference. The day before the keynote, she facilitated a pre-conference workshop. That evening after the workshop, she received news from the organizers that the conference the very next day was canceled. Saddened by the news, Carol and hundreds of attendees returned home.

At the same time, Katie was notified by both her children's school and her district that their doors would be closing as well. She, Carol, and many educators in the Western Hemisphere were now joining the ranks of full-time teachers in Asia and Europe who had found themselves transformed overnight into virtual teachers and, in many cases, homeschooling parents as well.

Districts and schools hurriedly sent students and teachers home. Educators rushed to assemble teaching materials to prepare students for distance learning. The more resourced schools had tablets and laptops for students to take home, while for many students, simply finding a reliable internet connection was a challenge. Disoriented, educators nationwide scrambled to figure out how to teach from their living rooms, kitchen tables, and even bedrooms to students learning in similar settings. There were far more questions raised than answered.

Some educators took to Twitter, Facebook, Instagram, and YouTube, desperately seeking guidance from countless platforms, and very quickly, a tidal wave of suggestions formed. Some teachers who used technology mainly for email found themselves in over their heads as they scrambled to incorporate new educational platforms to engage multilingual learners (MLLs) in ways they may not have used before in physical classrooms. Others who had traditionally viewed their profession as a solitary pursuit began gathering with small teams to collaborate virtually with other colleagues. Some districts and schools even engineered innovative services and outreach programs to serve their most marginalized families.

Many teachers emerged from this vertigo-inducing voyage completely transformed, viewing this time as a defining professional learning experience. If you were teaching in the spring of 2020, you undoubtedly recall the dizzying whiplash of rapid changes and contradictory guidance that defined the early weeks of the pandemic, necessitating the development of new skills and a willingness to embrace new approaches to serving culturally and linguistically diverse students.

Teachers around the world began to read and share articles, watch videos, listen to podcasts, attend webinars, and connect with colleagues on social media. The learning was efficient and essential, driven by the immediate need to serve students differently. This type of learning – situationally appropriate and immediately applicable, driven by personal choice, and designed to reflect individual styles, needs, and preferences – is a powerful and transformative tool for teachers not only in times of upheaval, but also in the most typical of circumstances. It's also exactly the type of professional learning for which we'll advocate in this book. Our focus rests on assisting teachers in selecting content that is personally relevant, can forge helpful professional connections, and can promote forms of participation that are comfortable for educators with different learning preferences.

We did not write this book as a response to the 2020 global pandemic. However, what we are sharing in this book speaks to what we all experienced and to the transformative power of personalizing our professional learning. Fortunately, you do not need another paralyzing pandemic to make professional learning personally meaningful. You simply need a guide to bring along with you on your learning journey.

PATHWAYS FOR PROFESSIONAL LEARNING

When we reflected on what has been working so well for us, especially in the context of remote learning, we realized that in many ways we were subconsciously following predefined best practices for educators interested in professional learning. Our learning paths mirrored some of the International Society of Technology in Education (ISTE) standards for educators (ISTE, 2018), with one standard in particular matching most closely with our methods:

1. LEARNER Educators continually improve their practice by learning from and with others and exploring proven and promising practices that leverage technology to improve student learning. Educators:

a) Set professional learning goals to **explore and apply** pedagogical approaches made possible by technology and reflect on their effectiveness.

b) Pursue professional interests by **creating and actively participating in local and global learning networks**.

c) **Stay current with research** that supports improved **student learning outcomes**, including findings from the **learning sciences**.

Our personal paths of professional learning were self-designed; we were not directed by our administrators to learn in this way. Our efforts were individual journeys driven by our own desires to improve our practices. As we each traveled on our individual paths, we stumbled upon each other and began to connect online. The three of us started following each other, sharing resources, learning together, attending the same virtual events, and celebrating each other's contributions to the field. Our relationship has since blossomed into a highly collaborative partnership where we work on projects together.

As we looked more into why our approaches worked so well for us, we began to realize that much of what we were doing was backed by research. In fact, key elements of our learning journeys were characteristic of an effective professional learning program (Darling-Hammond et al., 2009). We have since discovered that what we were doing also significantly mirrored and utilized aspects of D.R. Garrison's Model of Self-Directed Learning (1997). He proposed that adults become self-directed learners when they begin to manage and monitor their own learning habits and start to engage in meaningful activities for the sake of their own learning..

When the three of us met at the Seidlitz Education headquarters in the summer of 2019, we listed all the things we had been doing, individually and collectively, to grow as educators. Working together, we saw that our actions could be grouped into three categories that mirrored the language acquisition process. These categories became the primary sections of this book:

- **Interpretive Professional Learning:** listening to podcasts; learning from instructional videos; and reading books, research articles, blogs, infographics, and newsletters

- **Expressive Professional Learning:** designing infographics; presenting at conferences; and composing articles and blog posts

- **Interactive Professional Learning:** connecting with other educators on social media platforms; encouraging each other's successes; collaborating on projects; and engaging with other educators, authors, and researchers

The categories above align exactly with the domains of language we diligently work to develop in our multilingual learners. We can intentionally frame how we nurture and drive our own professional learning around this framework. Our multilingual learners need to listen, speak, read, and write to strengthen their language skills. Likewise, we have found that professional learning is more authentic and meaningful when we listen, speak, read, and write about our craft. This book provides various opportunities to engage in those four domains as forms of job-embedded professional learning.

Throughout the text, we've put together some ideas for potential next steps. Let's take the reading component of interpretive learning, for example, on p.27. To help you get started, we have provided different action ideas for teachers, coaches, and administrators:

> ## Try It Out!
>
> ### TEACHERS
> ☐ Subscribe to an educational newsletter.
> ☐ Find two or three blogs that spark your interest.
> ☐ Read a book that features characters with backgrounds that may be similar to some of your own students.
>
> ### COACHES
> ☐ Structure a meeting around an article from an educational newsletter.
> ☐ Share one blog post per newsletter.
> ☐ Share an infographic that is linked to an article during a meeting.
>
> ### ADMINISTRATORS
> ☐ Highlight an article of the week in a weekly email.
> ☐ Conduct an article discussion similar to a book talk during a meeting.
> ☐ Subscribe to an educational blog and commit to reading at least one post weekly.

OPPORTUNITIES FOR SELF-REFLECTION

In reflecting on the presented activities provided within these chapters, you will notice that all learning pathways will overlap in these common aspects:

- **Choice:** choosing the content, the process, the time frame, and the location of our professional learning

- **Continuity:** engaging in multiple experiences over an extended period of time

- **Community:** learning with other educators interested in professional growth

- **Connectedness:** studying relevant topics directly connected to your multilingual learners

- **Cost:** selecting learning opportunities that are compatible with your budget

Each of these aspects of professional learning differ based on your context. For example, you might work in an urban setting, or in a school building with many language specialists, or have access to a generous professional learning budget. You might even engage in activities that allow you to learn continuously throughout the year, such as an online book study for teachers of MLLs. On the other hand, it's possible that your district might not be able to provide many (if any) professional development opportunities at all.

You do not have to have all five aspects to have an enriching professional learning experience, we merely suggest that you view learning opportunities offered to you through these five lenses. If you are constrained in one aspect, look for another pathway through a different aspect. If you have several aspects, find ways to incorporate a few more into your experience. Your pathway is unique because of your context, so we want to empower you to be comfortable forging your own path.

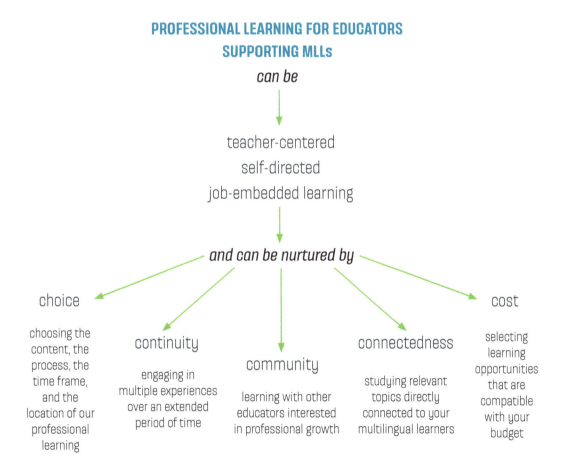

At the conclusion of each chapter in this book, you will use the graphic below to help guide your self-reflection on each of these five aspects. This functions as a series of dynamic scales that can be adjusted depending on your context and preferences. There is no right or wrong balance – all that matters is finding the balance that works for you. Some of the aspects, like the cost, for example, may be predetermined by someone else. For others, you might be free to explore the possibilities. In doing so, you can own your professional learning and make it work for you, your needs, and your life experiences.

DIRECTIONS

1. Choose a professional learning activity.
2. Evaluate that activity through the lens of each of these five aspects.
3. Mark on each line where the activity falls on the scale.

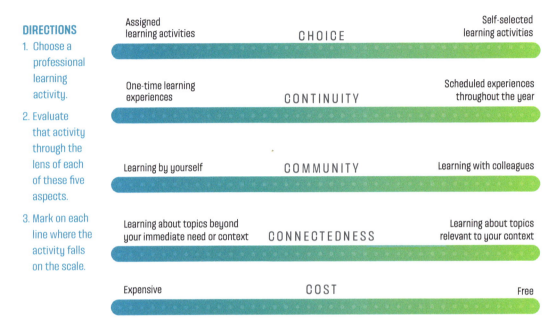

To the right is a sample of a completed graphic organizer to help you reflect on the concept and apply the suggestions to your context. We invite you to take time to think about all of the learning opportunities we present in the book and consider how you might be able to incorporate them into your life in a way that fits your schedule, budget, and access to the broader education community.

Example of a completed graphic organizer for the Interpretive chapter.

14 DIY PD: A Guide to Self-Directed Learning

We also end each chapter with a series of prompts to help you reflect on the content we have shared. You can use them as study questions or for self-reflection.

- **Describe** what you wish to gain from your professional learning journey.
- **Explain** how you could apply these five aspects to your professional learning journey.
- **Evaluate** how these would be perceived by teachers and principals in your district.
- **Explain** which one of the five aspects has had the greatest impact on your professional learning.
- **Analyze** the possible barriers to engaging in professional learning.
- **Brainstorm** ways to maximize any one of these considerations.

WHY WE WROTE THIS BOOK: WE SEE YOU

We have collaborated on this book because we see you. We see how some of you feel isolated as the only language specialists in your schools. We see you selling cookies and cupcakes just to pay for a conference fee and asking for donations from family members to cover the cost of a flight to attend a workshop. We see you sitting at a district-provided workshop on general education topics and wishing you had one geared toward working with multilingual learners.

We see school leaders, central office personnel, and superintendents, too. We see you looking at your shrinking budgets, scanning and rereading each line to find where you can take out a few more dollars to support language specialists. We see you cringing when opening an email from a teacher asking for support, pleading for funds to pay for a workshop. We see you scarfing down a sandwich as you dash between schools to set up after-school professional learning workshops. When the after-school workshop is over, we see you exhausted and melting into the driver's seat of your car, wishing you could do more.

We see all of you undaunted by these struggles, trudging through it all to learn on behalf of your multilingual learners. You are not alone. We have faced ...(and in fact *still* face) your exact professional learning challenges, yet we look at each other and look back at our own self-guided learning journeys and realize that there are scenic detours and alternative routes around many of these roadblocks.

The three of us have poured out our strategies and narrated our approaches in this guidebook so that you can chart your own professional pathway. Our paths have enriched our professional lives as educators, and we want you to experience the same energy, expansion, and exuberance that comes from owning your own professional learning.

We cannot wait to see all of you on this exhilarating path along with the three of us. Happy travels!

FIND THE AUTHORS ONLINE

Katie Toppel @KatieToppel | **blog** http://mllchatbkclub.blogspot.com
Tan Huynh @TanKHuynh | **blog** https://tankhuynh.com
Carol Salva @MsSalvac | **blog** https://salvac.edublogs.org

2

"The passion I am asking for from teachers is a passion beyond the pay cheque. It's a passion for children's books as well as for their own reading. For if teachers don't love to read, why on earth should children?"

Mem Fox, 2013

INTERPRETIVE PROFESSIONAL LEARNING

Katie's Journey

A few years ago, my colleague introduced me to the co-teaching model for teaching English learners. I was relatively new to being a language development specialist, and my only experience as both a former classroom teacher and as a language specialist, had been with the pull-out model. At the time, there was one school in my district that was already co-teaching and once I learned a little bit about it from a teacher who was involved, I wanted to know more.

She recommended the book *Collaboration and Co-Teaching: Strategies for English Learners* by Andrea Honigsfeld and Maria Dove (2010), which led me to purchase a copy and find the authors on Twitter. Little did I know that tweeting a picture of the book and saying I was going to start reading would lead to #MLLChat_BkClub! (For more about #MLLChat_BkClub, see the section called Independent to Interactive Reading on p. 78).

After reading *Collaboration and Co-Teaching,* I was sold on the idea of co-teaching and really wanted to try it. Since it was not the adopted model, my colleague (who had originally suggested we look into it) and I needed to seek permission to co-teach, which involved presenting our co-teaching plan to district leaders. We were really excited because the invitation to present our ideas seemed like an open door!

It's safe to say that when you get the opportunity to present to district leaders, you definitely want to make sure you're fully prepared. So, I set out to learn everything I could about co-teaching by finding as many resources and articles as I could get my hands on. The information and research included in those articles gave us valuable ideas and rationalizations to include in our presentation to support the case we were trying to make and we were able to lay out a plan and answer questions from administrators about our intentions and goals for how students would benefit from co-teaching.

Though we were granted permission to co-teach, opportunities for professional development or training were not readily available as co-teaching was not being widely used at the time. The resources we had gathered and read to support our request for permission also served as the content for our professional learning around co-teaching. In order to figure out what it would look like, we taught ourselves about the fundamentals of collaboration, the different models of co-teaching, and the collaboration and co-teaching cycle. We kind of 'built the plane while we were flying,' but we had a very successful first year because all of the information we got from the texts and articles we had read. Ultimately, we were able to expand our co-teaching program and the district is now working to systematize co-teaching because our leadership now sees and values the benefits. Subsequently, collaboration and co-teaching are now being embraced and utilized on a much larger scale within the district.

These efforts to learn about co-teaching by consuming existing material is an example of interpretive professional learning. This type of learning is also referred to as "receptive," though the term interpretive is a more accurate description of how people learn through receiving information. Interpretive learning offers a person the opportunity to listen to, read, or view materials and then use their own knowledge and experiences to arrive at a more complete interpretation of the content (CARLA, 2021; WIDA, 2020). This method of learning also provides an opportunity for us as teachers of multilingual learners to refine our practices by gathering the best and most recent information about professional topics related to teaching our students. We gather this knowledge through reading, listening to, and observing fellow educators, and comparing and contrasting their experiences with our own. This interpretive form of professional learning also includes reading, watching, and listening to a variety of other resources in order to process and retain new information.

Interpretive learning is an avenue through which we can be informed about changes in our ever-changing profession. We read, listen, and watch widely as a way to influence our thinking and better understand our evolving personal educator identities, including what we believe in, what we advocate for, and what current methods are most effective for the benefit of our multilingual learners. Every bit of new information is woven into our existing knowledge, always adding newer layers and deeper understanding.

One of the many benefits of interpretive learning is that while it can be done in community (as in book clubs and other group activities), it's also a powerful way to learn individually. As teachers, our investment in professional learning can be influenced by our beliefs about how we learn best. Differences in personality can also influence learning preferences and impact how motivated and comfortable (or uncomfortable) we feel in different learning environments. There may be times when we are excited to interact with others and take part in a shared learning process and other times when we prefer the focused energy that comes with working in solitude.

One-third to one-half of all people are introverts (Cain, 2012). Not to be confused with people who are "shy," introverts are people who prefer solitude as a low-key, quiet environment where they "engage in solo flights of thought" in order to maximize their talent, embrace their creativity, and experience revelations. Whether we think of ourselves as introverts or not, having "think time" to process new information before discussing it with others is as crucial for educators as it is for students, and interpretive learning offers plenty of opportunity for that to occur.

It's also essential that, as educators, we be critical consumers of our own professional learning. The following criteria, adapted from the International Baccalaureate Programme (2015), can be helpful to evaluate resources for interpretive learning:

Origin: Who is the author?

Purpose: What is the author's purpose for creating the content?

Value: What level of expertise does the creator/author have?

Limitations: Is there a lack of research-based evidence or citations, or does the creator have financial motives?

INTERPRETIVE LEARNING IS	INTERPRETIVE LEARNING IS NOT
- reading, listening, and watching	- focused on output or sharing with others
- reflecting internally	- identical for all teachers
- specific to individual needs & interests	- a linear process
- self-driven and/or self-selected	

READ

"We teachers have a huge responsibility to know our subject matter, our students, and our teaching. These three things are always evolving and it's our job to keep up with the changes" (Collins, 2004, p.3). Reading professional literature — just as you are doing now — is one of the primary ways we refine our instructional practices. The element of choice is a crucial component in making this approach successful for both students and teachers. "Choice has been identified as a powerful force that allows students to take ownership and responsibility for their learning" because it provides opportunities for autonomy and control (Gambrel, 2011, as cited in Boushey & Moser, 2014). In the same way that we encourage an element of choice in our students' reading, we as teachers also benefit from selecting our own texts to extend our own journeys in professional learning.

In a recent nationwide survey conducted by the National Education Association, teachers reported an overall lack of involvement in the decisions being made about their professional learning (Corwin et al., 2017, p. 2). Luckily, professional reading has remained one avenue for teachers to explore self-selected areas of focus. Educators can read to explore research regarding teaching culturally and linguistically diverse students, or they can read other types of texts that might offer explanations of strategies or instructional models, or provide examples of classroom applications. This can all be done independently or with a small cohort of colleagues.

Blogs

Katie's Journey

When I taught a course on assessment practices for K-12 multilingual learners at Portland State University, I ended the term by posing a challenge to my students. I asked them to think of a persisting question they had related to what we had covered in the course and then to do some research to deepen their knowledge and understanding around that topic. Topics could include project-based assessments, student portfolios, supporting students in self-assessment, or anything else from the course content that truly sparked their interest and was something they wanted to utilize in their teaching context.

In the directions for the assignment, I asked that they find two to three resources (e.g., websites, blogs, articles, or personal communication) that would help answer their question. It was interesting to see how students reacted when I mentioned blogs as a legitimate resource for a college assignment because they were so accustomed to long, in-depth research articles from the university library database that the idea of using educational blogs seemed questionable. However, educational blogs can often be a great resource for quality information.

for Educators of Multilingual Learners

Blogs differ from research articles in both tone and content. Bloggers often use a more personal voice in their writing while basing much of their content on their own individual experience and expertise. That's not at all to say that the content is necessarily devoid of research, but the way the content is presented is much more accessible and digestible, with an emphasis on the practical takeaways that teachers of MLLs need to hit the ground running. Blog posts generally tend to be shorter and more direct, with highlights that emphasize the most valuable information.

Educational blogs span a wide range of tones, from informal (e.g., descriptions of lessons, anecdotes about teaching, stories about students, recommendations for instructional materials, and ideas for classroom decor) to formal (e.g., relevant educational topics, ideas and advice, connections between best practices and current research). Both are valuable and useful, but it is important to use a critical lens when identifying both credible blog authors and content that best contribute to sound pedagogical knowledge.

Useful Blogs & Websites for Teachers of Multilingual Learners

ASCD in Service

Middle Web

Edutopia

Mindshift

Seidlitz Education

Larry Ferlazzo's Edublog

Colorín Colorado

Elementary English Language Learners by Valentina Gonzalez

Reflections on Teaching English Learners by Jana Echevarria

Inspiring English Language Learners by Emily Francis

Research

When selecting instructional strategies to use with multilingual learners, choosing practices that actually work is essential. There is a distinction between "research-based" and "evidence-based." Dr. Sally Shaywitz (The Yale Center for Dyslexia & Creativity, 2014) explains that to be evidence-based, there must be "proven efficacy." A practice or strategy is research-based if there are sound theoretical underpinnings but not necessarily evidence that proves the practice or strategy is effective.

As much as we love readily accessible platforms for receiving information, such as educational blogs and people in our Twitter professional learning networks (PLN), it is important to bear in mind that just because someone shares an idea or a lesson, it's not a guarantee that what they are sharing can be generalized as an effective strategy for language development across all populations of MLLs. The emphasis on research-based practices coincides with the need for a systematic, reliable, and precise way of documenting instructional practices in order to investigate effectiveness. It may be quicker and easier to read a few Tweets about great instructional ideas, but that should be balanced with a more in-depth look at what actual studies show.

Finding and reading research can sometimes feel daunting because there is so much out there, but primary sources can provide a lot of detailed and contextual information as well as concrete data around the efficacy of best practices for multilingual learners. Subscribing to a professional journal is a great way to stay informed about the latest findings and suggestions in the field and it's a guaranteed way to get quality information. Journals, available in both paper and digital formats, are published at different intervals throughout the year, with monthly or quarterly being most common.

Another way to access research articles that match our interests is to use Google Scholar Alerts. Because there is such a daunting amount of research available, we sometimes benefit from a way to funnel it down to what we need most. By entering keywords of interest and selecting alerts to be delivered via email, we can receive relevant articles directly into our inboxes.

Katie's Journey

When we first started writing this book, I signed up to receive alerts for articles about professional development and English learners. Almost daily, I receive an email from Google Scholar Alerts with hyperlinks to PDFs of the most recently published articles on those topics, and even though I don't always read the articles, I like knowing that I have easy access to the most recent information pertaining to topics that I am interested in.

Curriculum Documents

Many teachers skip straight to the lessons when working with a prescribed curriculum; however, teacher manuals and curriculum documents can often include great information. Identifying who authored or contributed to the curriculum also gives some insight into the underlying philosophies or instructional theories that the lessons are based on. For example, Dr. Nancy Frey and Dr. Deborah Short are among the program authors for National Geographic Reach, a language, literacy, and content program used for ELD instruction in districts throughout the United States.

Recognizing that authors whom you know and admire have contributed to curricula helps to contextualize the prescribed content because you know it is based on their extensive knowledge of best practices for multilingual learners. Also, teacher's editions are often embedded with research and instructional tips in callout boxes or support sections to help explain the instructional strategies or provide more detailed information about supporting students who are acquiring English at various levels. The teacher's edition likely includes a research base and bibliography which can provide a list of additional resources for a more in-depth understanding of any aspect of the curriculum.

These features may easily be missed, but they provide extensive details and information to help teachers better understand and meet the needs of their students. For example, among the additional resources included in one teacher's edition were:

- informational pieces about the stages of language acquisition
- guides to key terms, strategies, and activities that are included in the lessons
- language structure transfer charts, phonics transfer charts, and a scope & sequence for all the language and literacy concepts covered in the textbook

Newsletters

Subscribing to educational newsletters is a great way to have recent educational news, teaching ideas, articles, and links to additional resources delivered regularly to your inbox. The format of a newsletter provides the opportunity to view curated content and prioritize what to read about first.

Colorín Colorado is a bilingual site for educators and families of English learners that offers a weekly ELL Newsblast. It contains short descriptions of timely news with links to full news articles and a monthly T*ELL*E-Gram focused on a particular theme (see image on the next page). A plethora of information is available on the Colorín Colorado website itself while the newsletter package provides a more manageable amount of information in an organized list of easy-to-access resources.

The WIDA Consortium, ELPA21, and various state education agencies that have created common standards and assessments for students who are acquiring English also produce and distribute helpful newsletters as well. Some of the information contained in these newsletters pertains specifically to the ELPA21, ACCESS, or other state-specific assessments; however, they may also provide information on best practices for teaching multilingual learners. Newsletters such as these are helpful because they equip teachers with the opportunity to access high-quality information without having to search for it.

In the Classroom
Back-to-School Resources

Our back-to-school ELL resources include:

- New to Working with ELLs?
- Creating a Welcoming Classroom Environment
- Gear Up for a New School Year
- An ELL Teacher's Back-to-School Checklist
- Helping ELL Newcomers: Things Your Students Need to Know
- Welcome Kit for New ELLs
- ELL Parent and Family Outreach
- Ideas for Starting off the School Year from Larry Ferlazzo
- Strategies for Language and Vocabulary Instruction: Academic Vocabulary, Cognates, Language Objectives, and More!
- Updated Resource Action: Helping Colleagues Understand the Educator's Role

Video Clips: Advice for New ELL Teachers

Organizations that produce newsletters put in the time and effort to make sure they are presenting current, relevant, and useful information. This greatly benefits educators who may not have the time to spend perusing and evaluating the abundance of information that exists on different topics.

Newsletter example

Newsletters specifically created by practicing educators for other practicing educators are particularly valuable. These tend to highlight best practices for teaching multilingual learners in a fairly succinct and easily accessible manner. They also come with accolades from teachers or coaches who have used, observed, tweaked, and refined the practices in order to share the most pertinent suggestions. One example is a newsletter created by Michelle Gill, a teaching coach from Abbotsford, British Columbia, who puts together the concise "1-5-15" bulletin meant to provide educators with quick notes on relevant educational topics. Contained in each newsletter are items that take approximately 1, 5, and 15 minutes to read. Even for busy practitioners, this highly digestible PD presents a very practical way to learn.

for Educators of Multilingual Learners   23

Infographics

An infographic combines information and graphics in a "form of visual communication meant to capture attention and enhance comprehension" (Lankow, Ritchie, & Crooks, 2012; Ritchie, n.d.). Infographics are a fun, engaging way to access complex information or data that has been simplified so it can be consumed and understood easily by the audience (Mohamad et al., 2018). Concepts and information can be organized to illustrate "processes," "chronology," or "hierarchy" with images that connect to key ideas and help learners to remember (Ritchie, n.d.). Infographics are particularly useful because of their shareability on social media and their ease of use in an era marked by short attention spans and information overload (Smiciklas, 2012).

Aside from the clear visual appeal, the draw to infographics is the concise synthesis and organization of information to highlight the main ideas or salient points. The language of the eye and the language of the mind connect in a way that is magical and effortless because we can see patterns and connections that focus only on the information that is most important (McCandless, 2010). Infographics are usually presented in a user-friendly and easy-to-digest manner so that readers can access the takeaways without having to dig through lengthy texts. Additionally, infographic creators model how visuals, pictures, and icons paired with information are a great tool to support understanding and memory. Using infographics to learn in a professional context is a great way to remember that students who are acquiring English for the first time benefit when new information is broken down into more manageable segments.

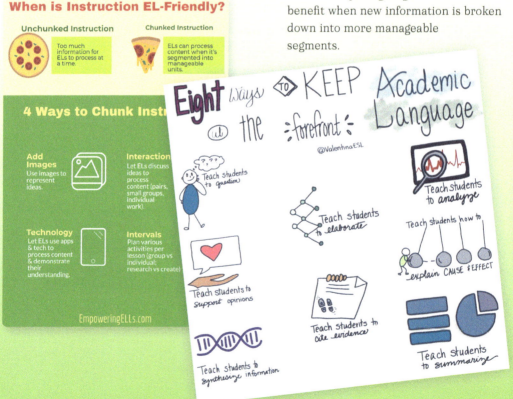

Recommended Sources for Infographics

SupportEd Infographics

E-learning ELL Infographics

Tan Huynh, Bathroom Briefs

Valentina Gonzalez, Infographics in English and Spanish

Larry Ferlazzo, The Best Infographics About Teaching & Learning English

Culturally Relevant Texts

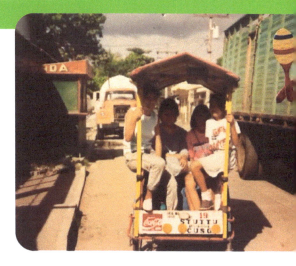

Filled with emotion and animation, Emily Francis stood on stage at the 2019 SIOP National Convention in Portland, Oregon, to share her story of coming to the United States from Guatemala as an unaccompanied teen with her younger siblings in order to reunite with her mom who had moved to the states several years prior. She shared how painful and challenging it was to tell her story. Like Emily, many of our students also have painful stories that they may wish to conceal out of fear, unfounded shame, or concerns about privacy. As we navigate relationships with students who may not be ready to share their personal experiences, it is helpful to lay a foundation for understanding by accessing literature featuring characters whose experiences mirror those of the students.

Reading novels featuring characters from diverse backgrounds and novels whose characters' lived experiences reflect circumstances faced

by students in the past or present day is a wonderful way to be more informed about students' lives. Rudine Sims Bishop (1990) initiated the metaphor of books as mirrors, windows, and sliding doors in an effort to shed light on the importance of multicultural literature. She emphasized that children need to be able to see themselves reflected in stories, but she also affirmed that literature additionally provides windows into different worlds and doors through which we can access different experiences from throughout our colorful and diverse world (Bishop, 2015).

Books serve as windows in the context of professional learning as well. As Tschida et al. (2014) explain, "To move readers beyond this ethnocentrism to view worlds that are not their own, books must also act as windows, allowing for a vicarious experience to supersede the limits of the readers' own lives and identities and spend time observing those of others" (p. 29).

Rudine Sims Bishop explains the power of diverse literature

Learning about circumstances that culturally and linguistically diverse students may experience can help teachers develop empathy surrounding the multitude of factors that are at play for students who are learning a new language. Through the vivid voices of characters (whether they are autobiographical, entirely fictionalized, or based on actual people), teachers can access insight and gain awareness about the experiences of refugees, migrants, and other immigrants who often navigate different identities at home and at school. These narratives also serve as powerful models for overcoming challenges for teachers and students alike.

Project LIT Community, a grassroots literacy movement aiming to empower readers and leaders in hundreds of schools and communities across the country, is a useful resource for finding novels that reflect diversity in authorship, characters, and experiences. A sizeable collection of such books compiled by teachers can also be found using the hashtag #AuthenticBooks4ELs. Here are some other recommended books for gaining perspective about multilingual learners:

- *The Circuit* by Franciso Jiménez, PhD: stories based on the author's experience as an undocumented migrant child

- *Refugee* by Alan Gratz: a story of three children living in different decades who escape their home countries because of political unrest, war, and economic hardship

- *Sylvia & Aki* by Winifred Conkling: a story about the effects of racial segregation on two third-grade girls in California following the Pearl Harbor attack and how this set the stage for the real life national reform that eventually lead to the desegregation of schools for Latino children

- *The House on Mango Street* by Sandra Cisneros: the story of Esperanza Cordero, a 12-year-old Chicana girl growing up in the Hispanic quarter of Chicago

- *The Name Jar* by Yangsook Choi: a picture book that addresses social identity through the story of a young Korean girl who starts to question her birth name when her new classmates have trouble pronouncing it

- *Front Desk* by Kelly Yang: a story that takes place at a motel in Anaheim, California, where Mia Yang, a 10-year-old Chinese immigrant, runs the front desk while her parents clean rooms

Electronic Versions

Electronic versions (or e-books) of these novels offer additional benefits for learning with features that complement the text, such as identifying which passages are highlighted most often by other readers. This provides an opportunity to stop and think about why so many people have chosen to select those specific sentences. Additionally, in most e-book apps, it's possible to add annotations to the text and highlight relevant portions.

It's worth mentioning that many novels can be accessed digitally for free through the library system. There are some apps through which library cardholders can borrow books from public library systems. Although wait times can sometimes be long, utilizing the library system for e-books can save a lot of money.

Try It Out!

TEACHERS
- ☐ Subscribe to an educational newsletter.
- ☐ Find two or three blogs that spark your interest.
- ☐ Read a book that features a character with a background similar to one/some of your students.

COACHES
- ☐ Structure a meeting around an article from an educational newsletter.
- ☐ Share one blog post per newsletter.
- ☐ Share an infographic that is linked to an article during a meeting.

ADMINISTRATORS
- ☐ Highlight an article of the week in a weekly email.
- ☐ Conduct an article talk similar to a book talk during a meeting.
- ☐ Subscribe to an educational blog and commit to reading at least one post weekly.

LISTEN

Listening plays yet another critical role in the learning process, serving as an opportunity to receive ideas, hear the viewpoints of others, and to consider them without the need to respond or interact. In our digital age, there is a wealth of information to be accessed audibly through all kinds of different media.

Education Radio and Podcasts

As of January 2021, there were over 1,750,000 podcasts and over 43 million episodes, with those numbers growing daily (Winn, 2021). Because podcast series feature episodes related to a particular topic, they're great for flexible learning since listeners can select specific episodes to listen to or subscribe for automatic downloads as new episodes become available.

Education podcasts can be found on a variety of platforms and through education radio networks. Podcast content ranges from discussions on thought-provoking topics to providing practical techniques for serving multilingual learners. One benefit to this method of learning is that it can be done while exercising, completing household chores, or driving.

Teachers of MLLs seeking a mentoring voice can often find support through the hosts of various podcasts.

For educators serving students who are acquiring English, this is particularly worthwhile since many report feeling as if they are working in a silo. A podcast by an educator with a similar experience or background can be a helpful reminder that there is a great deal of support and that as teachers we are not alone in our efforts.

The field is now brimming with podcasts for teachers of multilingual learners. As you seek out the right podcast, you'll find several types to support your journey, including the ones on the following page. Podcasts by a variety of stakeholders range from episodes about second language acquisition strategies to the importance of our stories as we strive to be culturally responsive and meet the social emotional needs of our students. At times, your professional learning may benefit most from hearing the reflections of a practicing educator, or at other times, you may want to listen to interviews with top experts in the field.

The DIESOL Podcast
Hosts: Brent Warner & Ixchell Reyes EdTech in ESL podcast: Digital Integration in ESOL.

The Highest Aspirations Podcast
bit.ly/HighestAspirations
Produced by Ellevation Education
Host: Steve Sofronas According to the website, Highest Aspirations includes conversations with educators and students, researchers and policy makers, and parents and community members about how to serve the ELL community.

Boosting Achievement: The ESL Podcast
bit.ly/BAPODCAST
Produced by voicEd Radio
Host: Carol Salva

VoicEd Radio
www.voiced.ca
Chief Catalyst: Stephen Hurley
Live Radio and Podcasts. Many podcasts are available on demand, and it offers radio streaming 24 hours a day. Live shows are also in the rotation.

Audiobooks

While many of us love to learn, we don't always have the time to sit down with a great book. Finding an audio version can be the answer for the busy educator looking to learn from an academic resource, a work of nonfiction, or even a novel.

Audiobooks have been around since Thomas Edison recorded "Mary Had a Little Lamb" on his invention, the phonograph (Rubery, 2017). The convenience of audiobooks makes them an appealing avenue for personalized professional learning. Just as with podcasts, they can be enjoyed while commuting or while doing errands. Teachers who find themselves thin on time but still want to expand their practice can turn chores and commutes into rich learning opportunities that can better align with their busy schedules.

Here are a few recommended audiobooks. Some of these titles have also been discussed during the virtual book club #MLLChat_BkClub, which you can read more about on p. 78.

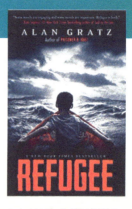

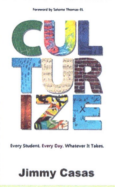
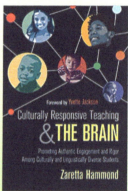
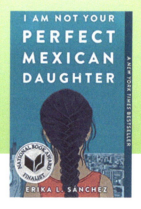
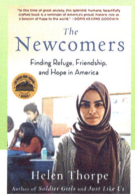

Carol's Journey

I have to admit that I love listening to books! Even when I have the print version in front of me and my eyes are tracking the words, I find it relaxing (and somehow more engaging) when I'm also hearing the words read aloud. I was a struggling reader as a child, so I'm sure there is a connection here. Whatever the reason, I have developed a love of finding Kindle versions of books and using the adaptive features from my mobile device to have the text read aloud.

Listening to Our Students

Using Text-To-Speech Technology

Any digital book can be turned into an audible learning experience through adaptive technology installed in smart devices, text-to-speech apps, and browser extensions. This technology, intended for persons with visual impairments, can be beneficial for anyone who would like to have their text read aloud. While the reading can be quite monotone and the commands may present a learning curve, the technology continues to improve.

Tan's Journey

My doorway is an extension of my classroom, and it is one of the places where I learn the most by listening. At the beginning of each class period, I stand at the door to greet my students. If a particular student is wearing her sports jersey on game day, I make sure to ask her how she is feeling about the upcoming match. If I walk in the hallway and see a particular student huddled with his friends as they show off their Magic: The Gathering cards, the next time he comes to my class, I will make sure to ask him what he likes about that game. I simply observe and ask non-threatening questions about a student's interests to get to know them better, allowing me to connect with each student and recognize their individuality. This not only shows that I want to develop a relationship with my students but also allows me to integrate their interests into my lessons if applicable.

Listening is an incredibly important communication skill, yet many of us struggle with listening well (Zwiers, 2019). The challenge comes not from a lack of opportunities to listen to others but in the ways that people listen. As Stephen Covey asks in *The 7 Habits of Highly Effective People* (1989), "are we listening to understand or are we listening to be understood?" He suggests that most people are listening with intent to reply versus an intent to understand. When operating from this response-centered mindset, it is easy to selectively hear things or misunderstand the other person's intentions.

Carol's Journey

I'm so grateful to have learned about Noa Daniel's *Building Outside the Blocks* projects. I have offered these optional projects to my students and I am always amazed at the time and effort students put into completing them. The majority of the work happens outside of class time, but it only takes five minutes to present when they are ready. These projects are a glimpse into their personal lives, and they are precious moments sprinkled throughout the year where we stop and really listen to each other. We all take a few minutes to hear and better understand the lives of our students as they stand before us vulnerably, but also beautifully strong and proud.

Sometimes additional distractions occur as messages are filtered through an individual's own life experiences and frame of reference and this interferes with our ability to truly listen to understand.

This skill of "listening to understand" is a critical one for us as teachers to develop in relation to our students for two important reasons. First, listening to students' stories about their lived experiences helps us to better understand them while ensuring that their experiences are reflected in the curriculum content. This is particularly important for our multilingual learners, who are often coming from a multitude of different backgrounds. Second, listening to student feedback about instruction is particularly useful for refining instructional practices to support students in the ways that are most helpful to them.

To effectively serve linguistically diverse students, it is important to focus on the assets they bring to our learning communities (Echevarria et al., 2017). Our classrooms are increasingly diverse, and it can be challenging for us to implement a culturally responsive teaching practice. One approach that helps is to provide a platform in our classrooms that enables us to listen to our students' voices. Providing students with such a platform enables us to draw from their funds of knowledge (Moll et al., 1992). As we become more culturally responsive through listening, we are better able to weave ethnic and cultural diversity into curriculum content (Gay, 2010). Deeply listening to our students enables us to leverage their cultural knowledge, prior experiences, frames of reference, and performance styles to teach them more effectively and build their intellectual capacity (Gay, 2010; Hammond, 2015). As we move toward "listening to understand," it becomes possible to structure collaborative learning environments where students are able to share their ideas, tell their stories, and contribute to discussions that are conducive to an active dialogue among all participants (Toppel, 2013).

Katie's Journey

At my school, we conducted empathy interviews for the purpose of hearing what students have to say and gaining a better understanding of what they think and feel about different aspects of school. When we did this, teachers came up with a set of questions to ask and then randomly selected some students for one-on-one interviews. When we sat down with students, we recorded their answers and then transcribed what they said in order to take a look at themes and potential areas for improvement. For example, we asked students what makes them feel successful at school and what makes them feel unsuccessful. We asked them to name an adult who cares about them and how they know that adult cares. This process was not only a great way to gather information from students, it was also really insightful and often touching. Hearing directly from students helped me set my sights on aspects of my teaching and student connections that I could improve.

An important part of this active dialogue is being open to hearing student perspectives about our own instructional practices (Toppel, 2013). Since teachers already continuously solicit information from students, it is the nature of the profession to ask questions and evaluate responses. There are benefits for everyone in asking students questions about their teachers' instructional practices. Students benefit from being in classes where all perspectives are heard and valued. Teachers benefit from leveraging the information students share to improve instructional delivery. Ultimately, an educator's professional learning is incomplete if students' voices are not represented.

Try It Out!

TEACHERS
- ☐ Search for podcast interviews given by authors of books you have read.
- ☐ Find an audiobook related to your professional context, and listen while doing an activity like laundry, exercising, or commuting.
- ☐ Use a voice messaging app to communicate with colleagues asynchronously. Share small sections of a podcast, and encourage group members to text comments and reflections.
- ☐ Have students respond to an anonymous survey, and then hold a class discussion to dialogue about the responses.

COACHES
- ☐ Find and listen to a podcast related to a current educational trend.
- ☐ Practice listening to understand when interacting with teachers.
- ☐ Review audiobooks that would make good suggestions for the teachers you support.

ADMINISTRATORS
- ☐ Before an invited author comes to facilitate professional learning, play a section of the audiobook for teachers to help form a connection between your staff and the author.
- ☐ Prior to a planned meeting, listen to a particular podcast episode and use the content to create a conversation starter for small group discussions at a staff meeting.
- ☐ Organize student panels or interviews to gain insight around student perspectives.

WATCH

Watching multimedia presentations brings together the power of auditory and visual learning, providing an enhanced experience for the learner in the same way that cooking shows magnify the knowledge aspiring chefs find in cookbooks. Clark & Mayer (2016) and Petty (2018) discuss the benefits of e-learning, and some of them align with the self-directed paths to learning discussed in this book:
• The flexibility to participate asynchronously
• Meaningful engagement with content
• Content tailored to individual needs
• The ability to self-pace

Webinars

Webinars can be a great way to access up-to-date information through a direct-teach format that often features opportunities for interactions that enhance the professional learning experience. Some webinars allow viewers to submit questions and comments upon registration while others encourage participants to answer questions or interact with each other during the webinar in a side chat.

The flexibility that comes with watching webinars is one of the format's greatest assets. Participants who are able to attend in real time may receive credit for continuing professional development hours if a certificate of attendance is offered. Interested educators may not be able to attend live for a myriad of reasons, even when the topic is of high interest. For this dilemma, many webinar hosts send slides and recorded video to registrants after the live session—so never hesitate to sign up anyway! Once the materials are received, they can be reviewed at the learner's convenience. As a bonus, participants are sometimes offered discount codes on books featured in the webinar presentations.

Numerous organizations offer webinars facilitated by researchers, thought leaders, and influential authors. When experts facilitate webinars, they are often free of charge, and the presenters frequently share some of the same content they are hired to deliver in person for thousands of dollars. While webinars first gained popularity as a marketing tool, they gained prominence during the COVID-19 pandemic as educators and professional developers alike scrambled to pivot their modes of instruction to provide quality learning content to both teachers and students.

At this critical juncture, most interactions were suddenly shifted to online exchanges, and in response, many education partners began offering webinars to support educators and other stakeholders. Searching a keyword along with "webinar" will now yield offerings from a diverse range of trusted sources such as local, state, and federal education agencies, professional learning organizations, research organizations, publishers, and industry organizations. These organizations often have the ability to bring in leading experts and scholars in the field to share their expertise.

Virtual Conferences

Attending educational conferences is an invaluable opportunity to learn about teaching multilingual learners from experts in the field, educators in the classrooms, administrators, instructional coaches, university professors, and authors. Conferences offer the opportunity to learn a substantial amount in a short time through a variety of sessions connected through a conference theme or educational focus.

However, conferences can also be quite costly. Travel costs in addition to registration fees can add up quickly, preventing some educators from being able to attend. Timing and location of conferences can be barriers as well. Luckily, there are now many virtual conferences that remove the physical, financial, and scheduling constraints that might exist for teachers of students who are acquiring English.

Virtual conferences provide the same opportunity to "attend" multiple sessions and hear from a variety of experts in the field, yet the content can be accessed digitally from anywhere in the world. This form of professional learning is sometimes referred to as "PD in your PJs" because attendees can participate without leaving the comfort of home.

To the right are a few examples of the many online conferences that have taken place in the past. As innovators in the field continue to reimagine professional learning, it is likely that the format of these opportunities will also evolve.

VirtuEL is a virtual conference co-founded by Tan Huynh and Carol Salva. Inspired by MADpd, Carol and Tan sought to emulate the "PD on the go" virtual conference format while providing content specifically focused on teaching and improving instructional practices for students who are acquiring English. Conferences include keynote presentations by experts in the field such as Nancy Motley (2017), Jana Echevarria (2018), and Andrea Honigsfeld and Maria Dove (2019) to jumpstart the learning.

MADpd is a participant-driven virtual conference organized by Derek Rhodenizer and Peter Cameron. The conference is hosted on YouTube and features half-hour or shorter video presentations by educators who wish to share one thing that makes a positive difference in their classrooms. The intent behind MADpd is that educators from all around the world can support one another and make a difference for students by sharing their personal success stories and ideas. While this conference is not specifically for teachers of students who are acquiring English, dozens of sessions are offered by language specialists addressing their specific needs.

English Learner Portal offers no-charge learning summits. The sessions are delivered through video by their own professional development team. They also offer professional learning and consultation services focused on the success of English learners.

Professional & Personal Videos

Watching teachers speak about their professional experiences or instructional practices is quite different from watching them in action. Unfortunately, teachers don't often have opportunities to observe and learn from colleagues when they are actively teaching, so watching videos of other educators teaching real students is a fantastic substitute. A teacher-created video blog (vlog) provides a high engagement, low-prep means of professional learning. Seeing how students engage with instructional tools, strategies, and content is a key component of professional learning because it provides the opportunity to really focus on what students are doing and saying during instruction.

When seeking videos of teachers delivering instruction, it is important to be clear on the learning goals these videos will support.

Watching another teacher interact with students has the most value when there is a clear goal as to what aspect of the teaching will best serve your own professional growth. To this end, short video clips modeling specific, high-impact teaching strategies can be very useful. It is also advisable to watch novice teachers as they often bring fresh approaches to classroom instruction.

This powerful form of professional learning meets the needs of teachers who are simply unable to spend a lot of time visiting other classrooms and other schools. Some of these videos have been professionally produced by nonprofits such as the Teaching Channel or education partners like Seidlitz Education, while others are created in-district by curriculum departments and other stakeholders to showcase methods and approaches that are effective for learners in that specific learning community.

Videos of teachers in action might also be available within your own district, produced by your own curriculum department. You may also follow an individual teacher online who has the proper permission to share instructional strategies from their personal video platforms or through social media.

Sometimes it is beneficial for teachers to see an entire lesson from start to finish, and other times it's helpful to watch a short clip that captures something powerful. Thankfully, hours of footage are now available to you and more videos are continually being added to the educational landscape.

Micro-Teaching

While the value of watching other educators in action is indisputable, there is also great learning potential in the self-reflection that results from filming one's own instructional delivery. This practice, known as "micro-teaching," was identified by John Hattie as one of the most effective practices linked to greater student achievement (2009). Micro-teaching was found to have double the average impact over other instructional practices, offering a significant incentive to overcome any shyness or reluctance that we as teachers might feel about viewing ourselves on video. Just as the National Council of Staff Development (2009), Center for American Progress (2012), and the Bill and Melinda Gates Foundation (2014) encourage teachers to frequently observe their colleagues teaching and reflect on their practice as a form of job-embedded professional learning, micro-teaching offers powerful opportunities to reflect on one's own practice.

In a research colloquium at Portland State University, Leticia Romero Grimaldo (2020), Principal Investigator and Project Director of Project ELITE[2], discusses the importance of self-reflective videos. She affirms the value of teachers being able to pause the video in order to look more deeply and think about what is taking place in the classroom at any point in time. Generating action items related to the targeted area for professional growth offers an additional form of self-reflection that is likely to result in more behavioral change.

To read more about the findings in John Hattie's research on micro-teaching, explore this article.

Many of us now have the ability to record our virtual instruction easily since there are now fewer barriers to this practice. For more information about using video for self reflection, refer to Laura Baecher's book, *Video in Teacher Learning: Through Their Own Eyes*.

Tan's Journey

I often engage in micro-teaching, and I use my tablet or computer to record a specific section of the lesson. For example, if I am interested in analyzing how I model a new procedure, I will record just that section, not the entire class. During break, a prep period, or lunch, I will review the video. A short recording is much more likely to be viewed than a longer one, because as teachers we are often too busy to view a 40-minute recording. Sometimes, I will record a long segment and fast-forward to different parts in order to watch certain components of the lesson to see the flow of the lesson, but these are rare occurrences.

TIPS FOR SETTING UP MICRO-TEACHING
- ✓ Talk to students about why you are micro-teaching
- ✓ Teach students to ignore the filming process and not to obstruct the camera
- ✓ Dim the screen brightness to prevent yourself or your students from being distracted
- ✓ View the recording as soon as possible
- ✓ Set the camera close to you so it will pick up your voice clearly
- ✓ Make sure the camera is not pointed toward a window as it will cast a shadow over your face

Micro-teaching is a wonderful job-embedded professional learning activity because it allows teachers to experience immediate improvement. When using this practice, our awareness shifts and sharpens, which can lead to greater achievement for all students but especially for our multilingual learners. The whole spirit of the approach in this book specifically (and of job-embedded learning in general) comes down to developing a heightened awareness of our practice. In that awareness, we will find the seed of teacher learning, growth, and development.

To take micro-teaching to another level, we can invite others to view and analyze the recording together. This less evaluative and much more collaborative reflection is one example of how we can take an independent professional learning activity and make it interactive, which we discuss further in Chapter 3.

Try It Out!

TEACHERS
- ☐ Register for a webinar, and watch it with the intention of learning at least one new strategy to apply in your classroom.
- ☐ Record one of your lessons to watch and reflect on areas for improvement.
- ☐ Watch a colleague teach a lesson live or on video with the aim of learning one new thing.

COACHES
- ☐ Gather a collection of similarly themed webinars to share with colleagues.
- ☐ Organize a webinar watch party where a group of teachers register and participate in a live webinar. Then schedule a follow up to discuss the ideas together.
- ☐ Share snippets from a single webinar over the course of several meetings.

ADMINISTRATORS
- ☐ Host your own virtual conference by compiling a variety of videos for staff members to watch.
- ☐ Launch the school year with a webinar that anchors the focus of that year.
- ☐ Negotiate with a consultant to hold a series of live webinars for the district over a period of a year.

Aspects to consider while reflecting on your learning.

DIRECTIONS
1. Choose a professional learning activity.
2. Evaluate that activity through the lens of each of these five aspects.
3. Mark on each line where the activity falls on the scale.

| Assigned learning activities | **CHOICE** | Self-selected learning activities |

| One-time learning experiences | **CONTINUITY** | Scheduled experiences throughout the year |

| Learning by yourself | **COMMUNITY** | Learning with colleagues |

| Learning about topics beyond your immediate need or context | **CONNECTEDNESS** | Learning about topics relevant to your context |

| Expensive | **COST** | Free |

REFLECT

- **Explain** which of the pathways (e.g., reading, listening, or watching) is your preferred approach to interpretive professional learning.
- **Describe** the barriers or challenges you encounter with interpretive learning.
- **Explain** some of the benefits of pursuing professional learning that is independent rather than group-oriented.
- **Evaluate** how different watching experiences can benefit your learning journey.
- **Describe** what you could do to better retain information while listening, reading, or watching videos.

©Seidlitz Education. All rights reserved.

3

"To understand is to invent."
— *Jean Piaget, 1980*

EXPRESSIVE PROFESSIONAL LEARNING

Tan's Journey

While I was an undergrad at Dickinson College, the career counseling office taped up their weekly newsletter in the bathroom stalls around campus. *The Toilet Paper* (aptly named) provided suggestions for internships, offered tips for resume writing, and announced future workshops. Students enjoyed these silly yet helpful newsletters.

Years later, while working at an international school in Laos, I wanted to offer quick strategies to support all teachers, not just my co-teachers. Meeting face to face with my colleagues was not an option due to scheduling constraints, and our weekly all-school meetings were not a viable option either because the content of the meetings changed each week.

One day, the thought of creating a version of *The Toilet Paper* that was focused on students who are acquiring English popped into my head. I set off to create weekly infographics to share one strategy per week. I called them *Bathroom Briefs: Strategies on the Go as you Go*. Each Saturday morning, I would run around to the faculty bathrooms on campus and tape them up. Most teachers giggled at these *Bathroom Briefs*, and on some occasions, they would even comment on how they enjoyed the strategies and applied them in their classes.

The first purpose of the *Bathroom Briefs* was to support teachers as they worked with students adding English to their language repertoire. As I created more and more *Bathroom Briefs*, the second purpose slowly emerged. In creating these whimsical infographics, I solidified my own list of strategies. When co-planning, I recalled these strategies more readily and adapted them more flexibly in multiple contexts. I became more of a resource for teachers by processing strategies I found effective, which prepared me to more clearly share them during planning meetings.

By operating at the "create" level of Bloom's Taxonomy, I more deeply understood second language acquisition strategies and was able to implement them more effectively with my students. The path from graphic creation to class implementation eventually merged. Over time, the practices turned into the belief that, with adequate support, our multilingual learners are capable of learning and achieving more than I had thought possible.

Even if only a few teachers looked forward to the *Bathroom Briefs*, creating them was a valuable process for me. Sometimes what we have created for others is actually what we needed to create for ourselves all along.

With expressive professional learning activities, we are at the center of the learning experience. Kolb & Fry's Experiential Learning Theory (1974) suggests that many adults learn best through a hands-on approach with an opportunity for reflection. Skills develop as teachers actively create by using their experiences and new learning. Through creating, we teachers can make sense of our practices and breathe life into pedagogical theories. Perhaps that is why the highest level of Bloom's revised taxonomy is "create" (Anderson et al., 2000).

Placing a premium on creation goes hand in hand with embracing the constructivist approach to teaching (Piaget, 1980; Elliott, Kratochwill, Littlefield Cook, & Travers, 2000). In this approach, teachers purposefully design learning experiences in which students are actively constructing knowledge to maximize their learning. Teachers can turn passive professional learning opportunities into active ones through this same approach by writing about them, creating visuals to process the ideas, and presenting evidence of implementation to fellow educators.

The chart below describes what expressive professional learning is and is not.

EXPRESSIVE LEARNING IS	EXPRESSIVE LEARNING IS NOT
- created primarily by the learner - potentially shared with others - crafted in the platform that's most appealing to the learner - brief or detailed depending on preference - helpful for stimulating reflections, clarifying practices, and documenting strategies - directly connected to the teaching context - collaborative if desired	- something that must be shared publicly - something that must be done collaboratively - something that must be done using technology - something assigned by others - an expensive activity

The expressive activities included in this section encourage teachers to self-reflect by:

- describing what went well for multilingual learners,
- identifying what did not go well,
- analyzing their own contributions during co-planning and co-teaching,
- rethinking the way language scaffolds are offered,
- evaluating how accessible assessments are for students,
- recognizing patterns in language attempts,
- questioning their beliefs about diverse populations of students, and
- examining potential implicit biases against linguistically and culturally diverse students and colleagues.

WRITE

One of the best ways to express your professional beliefs is through writing. Many teachers gain new insights and deeper understanding as they write about their practice (Burton et al., 2009). In the introduction to their book, Language Connections: Writing and Reading Across the Curriculum, Toby Fulwiler and Art Young (1982) write about the power of using writing to develop critical thinking:

We write to ourselves as well as talk with others to objectify our perceptions of reality; \ the primary function of this 'expressive' language is not to communicate, but to order and represent experience to our own understanding. In this sense language provides us with a unique way of knowing and becomes a tool for discovering, for shaping meaning, and for reaching understanding.

We'll discuss three options for writing here: journaling, blogging, and writing articles.

Journaling

While many young people keep journals, fewer adults seem to maintain job-related journals. However, Bailey points out that job-embedded journaling can be an effective tool for professional learning as it offers opportunities for educators to "experiment, criticize, doubt, express frustrations, and raise questions" (1990, p.218). Researchers suggest that journaling about teaching supports educators in deepening their professional expertise (Cakir, 2013; Deng & Yuen, 2013; Tang & Lam, 2014; Yang, 2009).

There are three layers of journaling as observed by Lee (2005):

- **Recall level**: writing that describes experiences
- **Rationalization level:** writing that looks for relationships between experiences to form guiding principles and transferable understandings
- **Reflectivity level:** writing with the intention of changing the future, analyzing experiences from various perspectives, and envisioning the outcome of instructional decisions on students, their behavior, and their achievements

Most teachers journal at the recall level (Lee, 2005). Unfortunately, merely recalling the events does not "necessarily lead to improved teaching" (Farrell, 2008, p.2).

Having a journal practice that includes a combination of describing events and thinking critically about them allows teachers to "systematically reflect on their own teaching and take responsibility for their actions in the classroom" (Farrell, p.2). Critical and reflective journaling enables teachers to locate patterns in past experiences and fully develop ideas for future instruction. Additionally, reading over past journal entries can help us recognize any biases we may hold or have held and show us how we've grown over time.

Journaling may be done before, during, or after a teaching or learning experience.

- **Journaling Before**

Journaling at the beginning of a lesson, unit, or important meeting can help set an intention for upcoming work or a goal for classroom instruction. Equally important, you can return to what you've written at a later date to examine how your thinking influenced your instruction.

- **Journaling During**

When engaged in a learning experience that spans an extended period of time, take momentary pauses in the process to reflect. Continuous reflection during a process can influence instructional decisions and approaches. This reflection will help shape instruction going forward.

- **Journaling After**

Journaling after an experience can reveal what it taught you about your multilingual learners, how they learn, and how effective various approaches were in teaching them. The sooner you journal after an event has occurred, the easier it will be to find the meaningful takeaways.

We know what you are thinking: How am I going to find time to journal? Journaling does not mean hours of writing. It might just mean investing ten to fifteen minutes at the beginning, during, or end of a unit in order to explore the transformative power of reflecting on our practices, our culturally and linguistically diverse students, and our beliefs.

Katie's Journey

When I was a student teacher, reflective assignments were a big part of my teacher preparation coursework. Part of submitting lesson plans to my advisor was writing post-lesson reflections in order to process what went well, what didn't go well, and what I would want to change for future lessons. In addition to student teaching all day, I was also taking evening courses, which meant I would often attend a class before I had a chance to sit down and write my thoughts about my lessons and my day at school. A large gap of time, with additional course content being introduced, created cognitive overload and made it hard to recall all the events in my day of student teaching. Something that helped me was recording myself talking on the drive home from school to capture my thoughts so that I could later listen back in order to process the day's events and write my reflections down. At the time, I had purchased a little handheld recorder, but that was before I owned a smartphone. Now, there are many voice recording apps available, making it easy to capture ideas and reflections on the go. If writing or journaling seems daunting, even the act of simply speaking thoughts out loud and recording them can contribute to meaningful reflections.

When I record journal reflections, I strive to uncover the link between my beliefs and my actions and how they impact the achievement of multilingual learners. In the process of journaling, the links reveal themselves.

Job-embedded journaling in our field means reflecting on your individual practices as well as collaboration with other educators. For multilingual learners in particular, it can be helpful to journal about the following things:

MLLs	**INSTRUCTION**	**COLLABORATION**
• How are students experiencing the class? • How are students interacting with their classmates? • How are students interacting with me and other educators? • How has trauma impacted students' experiences? • How are students with special needs being supported? • How are gifted students being supported? • How safe, welcomed, and affirmed do students feel in my class?	• How am I meaningfully integrating students' experiences and cultures within the curriculum? • How effectively am I using technology to scaffold instruction? • How am I differentiating instruction while maintaining high expectations? • How effective are my attempts to make content comprehensible? • What beliefs about students are most at play in my instruction? • What discoveries can I make from analyzing any assessments I have designed?	• What actions are nurturing positive professional relationships? • What actions might deteriorate my collaborative relationships? • How am I advocating for students' needs among my grade-level/subject area colleagues? • What approaches have I used to advocate for myself professionally? • How have some of my ideas, suggestions, models, or approaches been well received and why? • What impact do school-based systems have on my collaborative relationships? • (If you are co-teaching) How am I honoring my co-teachers' expertise?

This table offers a possible structure to support the journaling process. It includes elements of recalling events, a space to think critically about the event, and potential next steps.

PROMPTS	**RESPONSES**
Describe the event, meeting, learning experience, the upcoming project, etc.	
Identify your **feelings/thoughts** about it.	
Choose one **action** you can take after this journaling reflection.	

for Educators of Multilingual Learners 47

If you prefer not to handwrite, digital journaling is also an option. The following is a reflection from Rhonda Gadino, an elementary school language specialist in Kansas, on the impact of journaling as well as an example below from one of her digital entries.

> *I use journaling professionally as a teacher to reflect on my current teaching practices and to improve my lessons. After each lesson, usually at the end of the day, I write in my teacher journal about what went well, what didn't turn out as well as expected, ideas to improve a lesson, any "a-ha" moments, my goals for myself as a teacher, what I need to remember, and any concerns. This format helps me frame my reflections around the things that will make the most impact on my teaching and learning.*
>
> *Journaling has affected my instruction by making me more aware of my teaching practices and what works and does not work for my students. This daily reflection allows me to see my lessons for what they are and identify changes I can implement to make them better, which allows my students to learn even more. Being a reflective teacher allows me to develop and grow as an authentic instructor.*

Example journal entry from Rhonda:

Today's lesson was good but not great. The students were able to learn the objectives, but I felt like there was something missing from the lesson. When I thought about it, I realized that I forgot to have the students talk during the lesson. I had planned for a turn and talk but completely forgot about it. Tomorrow I am going to teach this lesson again and include student talk in more than one place. This is crucial for them as language learners. They have to use the language to learn the language. I will include a couple of sentence frames for them to have as a scaffold. I will also put sticky notes on my lesson plans that remind me to let them talk during the lesson in productive ways.

Blogging

If journaling could be compared to watching a movie at home, then blogging could be compared to going to the movies with friends. They both involve the exact same principles, but in two different environments. Job-embedded journaling is a private practice, while blogging puts your thoughts in public view. When we journal or blog to better our craft, we are writing to do the following (Ayas & Zeniuk, 2001; Downes, 2004):

- reflect on our teaching practice and pedagogical beliefs
- evaluate our approaches
- form understandings of teaching strategies and models

De Moor and Efimova (2004) suggest that edu-bloggers have two simultaneous conversations: one with the self and one with others. By intentionally sharing their writing with the general public, bloggers experience different opportunities for professional growth as teachers of multilingual learners.

Blogging can be a way to form a clearer teaching identity through sharing ideas and interacting with other educators (Gee, 2001). For example, to learn more about collaboration, you might blog about it. As you write publicly about your teacher collaboration, you could reflect on how you work with others. This reflection can reveal such insights as systems you employ, approaches you've formed, actions to avoid, and effective strategies. You can then share this information publicly with other educators even though you wrote it first for yourself.

Blogs can also be a great way to reflect on how our practice is informed by research. We can actively seek out and read peer-reviewed journals and other validated research to shape our practices, which we can then share on online writing platforms (Efimova & Fiedler, 2004). In the process, we may alter existing ideas, beliefs, and practices to become more effective.

MAINTAINING A BLOG

One of the greatest difficulties around blogging is being inspired to write consistently. "Where do you get the ideas for your articles?" is something we often hear. Creating categories can be a helpful way to maintain momentum. For example, Tan's blog contains articles in the categories of literacy, collaboration, WIDA, sheltered instruction, vocabulary, and technology. Once you've determined your categories, brainstorm a list of potential articles and then start writing. This approach lessens concerns around running out of topics to write about and helps sustain engagement with your blog, given that this type of ongoing professional learning is a significant characteristic of job-embedded learning (Darling-Hammond et al., 2009).

POSSIBLE BLOG POST STRUCTURE

Open with a **single teaching concept** and make sure to identify it clearly. Provide a **teaching story** to build context and ground the teaching concept. This can include examples from your personal experience.

Offer a **strategy** for language development, framework, process, or approach related to the teaching concept.

Provide a **takeaway** by concluding the article with a succinct paragraph that paraphrases your personal understanding of the teaching concept.

The informal nature of a blog can make it an attractive outlet for frustrations, but it is important to remember that fellow teachers appreciate positivity more than complaining, finger pointing, or negativity. Above all, we encourage you to resist the temptation to use the platform to call out individuals. This does not mean that you are not allowed to have strong convictions that might run counter to other beliefs; we simply suggest you adopt a gentle approach when communicating steadfast principles. As Warren Buffett is known for advising, "Praise by name, criticise by category." This means that we are never at liberty to criticize a person by name in our blog. It is better to use hypothetical, contrasting examples (one using best practices, one not) to express critical views of a particular practice.

Katie's Journey

When I was a kindergarten teacher, I was an active edu-blogger. At one point, I went through some growing pains when my administrator indicated that I needed to work on classroom management. This was a time in my career when I went home and cried daily because I felt like a failure. I used my blog as a way to sort through my emotions around feeling "criticized," yet I was very cognizant of the fact that I was putting my words "out there" in the blogosphere. I recognized that I would be mortified if I wrote negatively about my administrator and she were to read it. So, when I composed my posts, I chose my words very carefully, almost as if I were writing to my future self with a focus on what I could learn from the situation. I have gone back and reread those posts and am proud of the way I processed the moment in my teaching career when things weren't going well.

Here is an excerpt from one of my posts:

> Although I don't want to be someone who needs help, I do recognize that as teachers we are always trying to improve, and there isn't a teacher out there who couldn't benefit from interacting with more teachers, learning from other teachers, or getting some input from other teachers. As much as I am sad about not being the 'perfect' teacher, I know that this experience will have a good outcome if I acknowledge the importance of learning from others, suck up my pride, reach out for help, and accept the support of other teachers who are willing to help me. This sure has been a humbling experience, but I am a firm believer that everything happens for a reason. I would rather have a very active principal who watches me teach and offers support when needed than a principal who is not at all familiar with what my classroom is like and how I teach.

Here are a few other expert edu-bloggers' thoughts on the importance of blogging as a professional development tool for teachers.

I'm a big fan of teachers writing blogs as a key part of their professional learning! I began writing mine 13 years ago. I had been collecting online resources for my students — both English language learners and English-proficient students who I taught in "intervention" classes — and thought that other educators might find them useful in their classrooms too. A blog seemed like a good way to share those resources with the world.

After a while, however, I began to see a blog as much more than just a place to store links to resources. Just as we teachers tell our students that writing can help develop and clarify thoughts, I found that writing about my classroom experiences and questions I had about them (never identifying individual students and never "complaining" about them, either) helped me reflect on my practice and made me a better teacher. In addition, readers' reactions to my posts helped me even more!

Writing regular posts also motivated me to be aware of what other educators and researchers were doing around the country and pushed me to think more proactively about how I could apply their experiences to my own classroom.

My blog has also provided colleagues and talented educators from throughout the country with a vehicle where they could share their own ideas and, in some cases, provided a "jumping-off" point for them to begin their own blogs or other regular public writing practices.

Finally, writing the blog has created opportunities for me to expand my writing horizons into other periodicals and in authorship of books. Developing the self-confidence that what I had to say was of interest and of help to others encouraged me to push myself to step up to those more intellectually challenging pursuits, and they too have made me a better person and a better teacher.

Larry Ferlazzo
High School Educator, Author, Radio Host, and Education Blogger

I started my blog at first as a reflective tool. Writing was a way for me to document my methods and pedagogy as I practiced and learned. I wrote candidly, exempting myself from writing "articles" and instead writing about real experiences that I had cultivated in the classroom. As I shared my writing, others in the teaching community took interest. I started forming connections with many of these individuals, both online and in person at conferences. We'd talk shop, share resources, and help each other problem-solve. Blogging has helped me expand my professional network internationally. I went from being on an "island" to being on a massive continent!

Justin Garcia
Teacher, Author of "Adventures in Teaching" blog, Creator of #Queer_edchat

The act of trying to put ideas into words for an audience creates a different level of accountability and pressure than you'd get by just writing privately for yourself and thinking your own thoughts. It's the same way that talking to a friend can really crystalize how you feel about something or what your ideas are.

Blogging can also help writers learn. Through my blog, I try pretty regularly to back up my writing with research. I have ideas that I feel have worked, and I get ideas from teachers, but ultimately, I want to research those ideas and prove them to be true. That level of accountability forces me to learn on a deeper level than I would if I wasn't writing for an audience.

Finally, keeping a blog over time gives you a record to look back on. Not only does this show you your growth, but it can remind you of things you've learned in the past, bringing them up to short-term memory. Then you can use these things in different ways than you would have when you first learned them.

For most teachers, the benefit of blogging is that extra level of processing and reflecting. There are so many distractions and ways for your brain to stay busy throughout the day that blogging is almost a meditation, forcing you to focus, dig deep, and reflect.

Jennifer Gonzalez
Founder & Editor in Chief, Cult of Pedagogy

Vlogging

Similar to the benefits found in reflective journaling or blogging, when you record a video message as a vlog, you can deeply process and internalize key principles of instruction. Vlogging refines and hones your teaching practice further because you are required to think about what you did, the effects on learning, and your future steps. The next level to this is simply to record a short, two-minute part of your lesson and share it on social media. By doing this, you invite a wider audience of teachers to help you reflect on your practice as well as stimulating you to reflect on your own. You might prefer vlogging if you do not have time to sit down and go through the writing process, as you can simply record and share on your channel with minor editing needed.

While this section offers ideas, examples, and ways to structure a blog, it is important to keep in mind that there are no specific rules to blogging. Learning opportunities exist whether the writing is a focused, research-cited entry or a free-flowing stream of ideas. Those casual reflections might be the first step toward something more formal, but they still serve as a tool for professional learning, which is the intended goal of the activity.

Writing Articles for Organizations

Guest posting on other teaching blogs and writing for professional organizations can be an easier entry point than establishing your own blog. It is like dipping your toes in the water before diving in headfirst. Just like journaling and blogging, guest posting for others can spur self-reflection, and being a reflective practitioner is an indicator that a teacher provides high quality instruction (Farell, 2015a, 2015b; Finlay, 2008; Priddis & Rogers, 2018). Guest blogging or writing articles can also refine your practice in two ways:

- Other bloggers, and especially professional organizations, may have guidelines or a set structure for writers to follow. This can help to focus your reflection while providing tips for structuring a blog of your own.
- You get to interact with a broader audience who may provide feedback that can expand your craft (Downes, 2004; Luehmann, 2008).

It is not necessary to wait to be invited to guest post for an edu-blogger. If there is an edu-blogger who you admire and respect, ask them if they welcome guest blogging. List topics you are especially positioned to talk about or issues you want to advocate for.

Another blogging opportunity is to write for professional organizations, teaching associations, education-focused media outlets, and education companies. These groups may run conferences and/or publish newsletters, blogs, and journals.

Educational Writing Outlets to Consider

Education Week	WIDA
Edutopia	SIOP
ASCD	NCTE
ELLevation	TESOL
Seidlitz Education	ISTE
Confianza	Mindshift
Colorín Colorado	Education Post

Professional organizations often publish the work of experts, but they also want to hear from practitioners who can contribute a crucial classroom perspective. Seek out credible organizations that are publishing quality content you admire, and find out about their process for selecting guest authors. By sharing your message with their audiences, you'll have the opportunity to grow your network and tap into other experts' insights and experiences to augment your own.

Tan's Journey

Software companies present another opportunity to guest blog. I was once struggling to help a language learner with selective mutism communicate beyond a simple nod or head shake. In one particular class, students were reading about the ancient Athenian education system. I offered this particular student a presentation platform called Buncee as a way to communicate his understanding in a less threatening medium than an essay, which was the original assignment. Ten minutes went by and I checked in on this student to find that he had used the presentation app to draw what Athenian education might have looked like as well as writing out a sentence to explain the drawing.

I was so thrilled that the student used Buncee's platform to give himself a voice that I posted about it on Twitter while tagging Buncee. Later, Buncee invited me to share this experience on their blog. If there is a particular app or platform that you use to innovate instruction for MLLs, contact them to see if you can contribute a post to their blog. They, too, appreciate stories of successful application of their products.

Every educator can benefit from learning to blog because it uses many of the same "muscles" that teaching does. The end goal of teaching and writing for an audience is, in some ways, the same: to impart a lesson or knowledge that helps someone grow. There's a huge audience of other educators who are hungry to share their experiences and learn about the experiences of others. If you're interested in writing guest blogs, take some time to think about topics you can offer insight on and the issues you're really passionate about. Ask yourself what perspective you can provide that's better than anyone else's. Read blogs often and reach out to editors of the blogs you admire. Developing relationships is key. And when it comes to the writing itself, you can approach it in the same way that you plan a lesson. Select a topic you know about and are interested in, plot out the points you want to get across, and dig in. Your blog should make its points clearly and be concise (never lengthy just for the sake of being lengthy). One more thing: Be sure to find a good editor — someone who can critique not just your writing but the content itself. Over time, a good editor can improve your writing, not just fix a single article.

Alexa Epitropoulos
Media and Author Relations Specialist at ASCD

Larry Ferlazzo's Recommendations for Guest Posting on Blogs

1. Try to become very familiar with what the site generally publishes.

2. Leaving thoughtful comments on blog sites is definitely a great way to become known by the blogger or site manager. For my Ed Week column, I will often ask people who comment on posts to write formal responses.

3. I think everybody is interested in examples of Teacher Action Research, where teachers have tried to put some new type of teaching into place and have designed a system to evaluate its effectiveness.

4. Writing a guest post is an excellent way to improve your writing skills, especially if you make it very clear you won't complain if your piece is edited.

Try It Out!

TEACHERS
- ☐ Start a 10-minute daily journaling practice.
- ☐ Journal as a form of reflection at the end of a unit.
- ☐ Blog about a particular teaching experience.

COACHES
- ☐ Pick a particular grade or content to journal about.
- ☐ Share select aspects of your journal with teachers whom you support.
- ☐ Journal before and after making a decision.
- ☐ Choose particular teachers who you want to guide in creating a blog.

ADMINISTRATORS
- ☐ Identify teachers who are already journaling, and ask them to share their experience during a meeting.
- ☐ Journal for one month on a particular issue.
- ☐ Share select aspects of your journal with teachers whom you support.
- ☐ Blog about a new initiative.

CREATE

The creative process enlists critical thinking skills that challenge the learner to think deeply in order to represent their learning in an innovative way. In the most updated version of Bloom's Taxonomy, we see that the highest level of learning is creation, with the learner putting elements together to form a novel, coherent whole, or making an original product (Krathwohl, 2002). Critical thinking can involve finding patterns, understanding relationships, critiquing, evaluating, analyzing, or making decisions with regards to the new information that has been acquired. The act of creating can be individual or collaborative and requires a shift from basic comprehension to utilizing information for more complex purposes.

Creating can be focused on furthering personal learning, or it can provide an opportunity to reflect on, synthesize, and possibly simplify content in order to share learning with others. By sketching out an illustration or utilizing technology to visually represent our thoughts, we are creating. Creating involves many other levels of learning in order to plan and produce something new.

Graphics

For some, sketchnoting and creating infographics are two forms of professional learning that support deep synthesis of complex ideas and details. These practices help busy educators maximize professional learning whether they have taken time off from teaching to attend a workshop or used personal time to read a professional resource.

Sketchnotes

Sketchnoting is an innovative option for capturing notes by drawing images – digitally or by hand – that represent concepts and ideas gleaned from professional learning activities. This process involves synthesizing information by using a combination of images and limited text that can support a deeper understanding of information and increase retention (Fernandes et al., 2018).

According to the picture superior effect theory, pictures have a higher recognition rate than written words (Paivio & Csapo, 1973) as up to 75 percent of our cognitive system is devoted to our vision. Paivio suggests that when we see a picture, it is encoded in our brains twice – once visually and once verbally. This process is called dual-coding. When we take visual notes, we process the information deeply as the content is being encoded both visually and verbally.

The "Drawing Effect" is a concept that refers to the power of drawing as a way of processing information (Wammes et al., 2016). In their experiments, Wammes et al. provided a set amount of time for two groups of participants to rewrite certain information over and over again. In one group, the participants were given the same amount of time as the other group but were asked to draw the information. When both groups were given a memory test, the researchers found that the drawing group was able to recover significantly more information with greater details and connection between ideas.

Sketchnoting can also be used to deeply process ideas learned during a conference, from reading an education-related article or book, or from watching a pedagogy-related video.

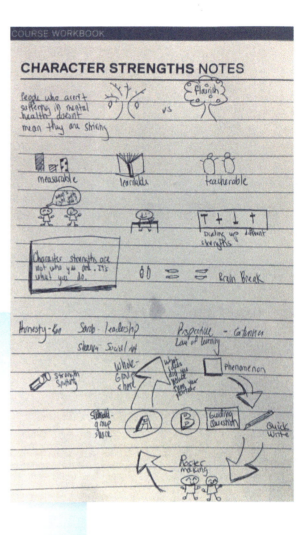

Tan's Journey

At one of my previous schools, I attended a two-day workshop on positive school psychology. I wanted to be more focused and process the information much more deeply, so I drew the most important ideas as shown in the image here. The sketches were not of high quality, but they did not need to be. The process of sketchnoting during the workshop was more important than the quality of the drawings. As I reviewed my sketchnote months later, the ideas easily came back more readily than they would have if I'd reviewed a full page of bulleted notes.

Katie's Journey

I have a confession. I have a terrible memory. I love to read, and I read so much, but it's challenging to keep track of my biggest takeaways from all the amazing books I've read over time. When I read professional texts, I have started to use sketchnoting as a way to capture the salient points that I really want to remember and use in my teaching. As I read, I highlight the text and make notes in the margins. Then when I have finished the book, I go back and look at what I marked in order to create some visual representations and capture the essential ideas. Pictures really help me remember, and it is so much more feasible to flip back through my notebook and look over my sketchnotes to recall what I've learned as opposed to flipping through long texts to try and pinpoint where I read about something. Sketchnoting provides me with an extra layer of reflection after reading, which is what I need in order to really process what I've learned.

As an avid sketchnoter, I find that this method has many benefits for both the sketchnoter and its viewers. As the sketchnoter, creating increases my engagement in learning and my depth of understanding. There are two ways this happens for me:

Often before I begin writing, my mind leads me to think visually first. The ideas come to me as images, and I draw them out. As I sketch, I add keywords to the images. This becomes a sketchnote because it includes both linguistic and nonlinguistic representations. Sketchnoting forces me to be intentional about what's important and how to organize ideas. Only later do I write about the topic. I use the sketchnote as a form of outline for my writing.

Other times, while I'm reading or taking in information from watching a TEDtalk or at a conference, I enjoy taking sketchnotes to allow my brain to process what I'm thinking as I'm learning. I find that if I don't sketchnote, I become passive, and my recall of the information decreases. You may be wondering why I don't just take traditional, written notes. The reason is that by pushing my brain to come up with relevant images, I am synthesising information and analyzing ideas.

Valentina Gonzalez
*Sketchnote Artist, Author &
Educational Consultant for Seidlitz Education*

Infographics

If you like sketchnoting, infographics might be another option to consider for sharing strategies and insights. One major distinction between infographics and sketchnoting is that sketchnoting is more for processing ideas and information, while infographics are created mainly for audiences to consume. However, there is also tremendous value in creating them.

There are many ways infographics can be used as job-embedded professional learning:

- Sharing ideas from a recent book you read that pertains to working with multilingual learners.
- Communicating ideas from a webinar about topics related to language acquisition.
- Depicting a process, principle, or a protocol that supports language development.

If you can create a graphic organizer for students, you possess all the necessary skills to create infographics. You do not need artistic skills to create informative, visually appealing infographics. I create my graphics in Google Drawings. I drop my content into text boxes, sprinkle in labels to section off different ideas, and play with the layout, intentionally leaving room for white space. Finally, I insert icons to match the infographic's content. My only expense is a subscription to an icon database, which I gladly pay for since the icons are essential to the readability of an infographic. – **Tan**

Formative data comes from anything students:

Move
- point to
- objects
- their bodies
- manipulatives
- picture / word sorts

Create
- models
- drawings
- infographics
- animated videos

Say
- key content-specific verbs, nouns, adjectives, verb
- repeating key words
- in their home language

@TanKHuynh

Write
- copy or recreate
- label a diagram w/ content-specific nouns, verbs, adjectives, adverbs
- cloze passages
- outline/graphic organizer
- home language

BookSnaps

If infographics seem intimidating, then a manageable first step might be to create a BookSnap. This idea from Tara Martin (n.d.) involves using a smartphone to take pictures of particularly though-provoking or helpful parts of the reading as a form of annotation that does not leave a mark on the text. Photo-editing programs can then be used to annotate the images with text boxes, emojis, and other graphics such as stickers and Bitmojis.

BookSnaps serve two purposes:
1. To support processing of the text
2. To share your thinking about the text with your learning community

Creating BookSnaps is an engaging and active way to synthesize understanding.

Try It Out!

TEACHERS
- ☐ Create a graphic showing a strategy from your content area or grade level.
- ☐ Sketchnote the ideas presented during a training.
- ☐ Create a BookSnap from a book you are reading to remember a key point or quote.

COACHES
- ☐ Sketchnote how a department, grade level, or school is dealing with a particular issue.
- ☐ Sketchnote a unit's enduring understanding and guiding questions.
- ☐ Create a vlog or video series to share strategies related to a particular language domain.
- ☐ Create a digital graphic with linked professional learning options.

ADMINISTRATORS
- ☐ Create graphics for particular audiences (e.g., principals, coaches, community, boards).
- ☐ Sketchnote the ideas presented during a meeting.
- ☐ Create a BookSnap from an article or a book by a consultant who is coming to the district to provide professional learning.
- ☐ Share a video for teachers to view before attending a meeting.

PRESENT

Delivering and reflecting on a learning experience that you have designed for others offers a vast number of benefits to both the presenter and the audience. The ripple effects of these presentations may reach many educators, which in turn benefit countless numbers of students both locally and around the world.

In early 2018, I was encouraged by Carol Salva to present at #MADpd's virtual "unconference." I made this decision to present even though I'd never been part of a live streamed event before.

As I prepared for the day, I communicated to Carol that I was very nervous about the technology aspect. She assured me that things would work out just fine and reiterated that there were too many positive outcomes for the presenter, for potential viewers, and for students to not give it a shot.

The day came and, as luck would have it, my technology did fail! I was not able to get my audio working during the livestream, and after some attempts to resolve the issue, I logged off, embarrassed and disappointed.

In those first few hours, all I could do was shudder and think, "See? My worst nightmare came true. I failed!" But as the hours and days passed, I came to see it differently. You see, this is not the end of the story. Carol had attended my session and was the one to alert me that my audio was not working. She helped me troubleshoot until I was able to record the video and upload it into the lineup of presentations, where it was viewed on replay by more than 100 teachers and remains accessible to this day. What initially had seemed like defeat quickly changed to lasting success. (Use this QR code to check out that video.)

In presenting, we all take a risk, but the presentation is professional development in and of itself. It is how we grow and learn as educators. And ultimately, this is what we want for our students — to see that, as Henry Ford famously said, "Failure is simply the opportunity to begin again, this time more intelligently."

Jennifer Hunter Dillon
ESL teacher, Thames Valley District School Board;
Professor of Education, Western University

Why Present to Other Educators?

GROW IN OUR CONFIDENCE

Like Jennifer, many of us have been nervous about presenting to other educators, whether virtually or in person. Whether the concern is about technology, about public speaking, or even a little bit of imposter syndrome, the reality is that we all have something to contribute, and we all have a lot to gain from sharing our knowledge in this way.

It is common to feel fearful about presenting to an audience, but it can be helpful to remember that failure is not the enemy. In fact, failure is recognized as a key component of any learning journey. Ironically, as much as educators encourage students to take risks that might result in failure, we are often not so eager to experience failure ourselves. This is understandable, but think back to Jennifer's story. Were there real risks in presenting to a live audience? Yes. Was she fearful? Yes. Did she experience a failure? Yes. But was this a huge success in the bigger picture? Yes! Jennifer could have thrown in the towel and walked away when her technology failed her. But she didn't! She persevered, displaying grit and a growth mindset about the task at hand.

Stage fright and technological mishaps aside, novice educators often fear they have not mastered enough pedagogy to present to others, but that is simply not the case. In fact, this may be the ideal time to begin. Derek Rhodenizer and Peter Cameron, founders of #MADpd, specifically recruit new educators for their online "unconference" because they believe that everyone has at least one thing that is making a difference

> **NEW PRESENTER TIP**
>
> If you want to deliver a low stress, high impact presentation, consider offering a "Lessons Learned" session around a new strategy or initiative you have tried. What were your lessons learned? How did you reset, and what eventually worked? Hearing how a fellow professional found success with anything from designing a mini-lesson to developing an after-school program is valuable for our field.

for students. Their online conference was founded on that principle. Remember that not everyone knows what you know, and don't assume that your colleagues can't benefit from hearing your voice on any particular technique, strategy, or idea. All educators benefit from fresh eyes and new perspectives.

GROW OUR OWN KNOWLEDGE

Furthermore, no matter how experienced or novice you are, there's always more to learn. *Docendo discimus* is a Latin proverb that means "by teaching, we learn." The idea of improving mastery by teaching another person is not a new concept to those of us in the field of education. Many teachers see positive outcomes of peer-to-peer teaching in their classrooms on a regular basis. We know when one student is tutoring (or teaching), the other student is reaping a great deal of benefits from the exchange. Research has shown that preparing to teach, coupled with actually teaching, can lead to greater long-term learning (Fiorella & Mayer, 2014).

Although delivering professional development to a live audience differs from the experience students have when they teach a new concept to others, it offers many of the same rewards. This phenomenon is known as the "Protégé Effect." Why does the act of teaching another person lead to so much growth for the person doing the teaching? In his 2019 blog post entitled, "Mastering the Protege Effect: What Decades of Experience Teaches us About Learning," education blogger Reed Rawlings explains:

- Teaching a subject means you've got to take on a different perspective and think about fundamental issues more abstractly.
- Teaching forces you to think critically about an issue.
- When you're teaching, there's an enhanced fear of failure.
- This fear can act as both an extrinsic and intrinsic motivator, prompting you to fine-tune your learning.
- You'll use different, better tools when teaching. There are a host of options, and committing to teaching allows you to explore each of them.

Additionally, presenters can enhance their own learning by taking some time afterward to reflect on what was effective and what could be improved. According to Hattie (2009), reflection and evaluation have a significant effect on learning. Identifying areas of focus for adjustment is an essential and natural step in the process of life-long learning.

GROW OUR PROFESSIONAL LEARNING NETWORK

Leading a professional development session also offers the opportunity to connect with other educators of multilingual learners from a place of common interest. Growing a network of similarly situated educators can be a powerful way to expand your self-directed professional learning. As you present to local, national, and international audiences in person or online, each experience provides you with an opportunity to connect to more educators. Weinberger (2014) suggests that no one person, regardless of how much knowledge they have, will be as knowledgeable as everyone working together. Often the "smartest person in the room is the room," and wouldn't you want your room to be filled with other professionals whose interests and expertise align with yours?

TYPES OF CONFERENCES THAT OFFER EDUCATORS OPPORTUNITIES TO PRESENT

District conferences	These may offer interactive learning opportunities, they are usually free, and they cater to the schedules of the district staff. If you do not find interactive learning opportunities at a district conference, you might think of offering an interactive session yourself. District organizers may be receptive to teacher presenters or teacher-led discussion groups.
State, regional, and local conferences	These conferences offer many of the same benefits as national and international conferences, but travel costs are manageable and they allow you to participate in learning about local issues.
International and national conferences	These draw more experts in the field but have the highest registration fees and may require substantial travel costs.
Virtual conferences	Conferences now exist online and on demand. Virtual conferences can remove the physical, financial, and time barriers for teachers of multilingual learners. You can "attend" a conference when it happens live or watch sessions on-demand afterward. Watching the live conference offers the most interactive experience, as presenters interact with participants during their presentations.
Unconferences	These are designed to provide participant-driven professional development. The sessions are determined by the participants at the beginning of the conference.

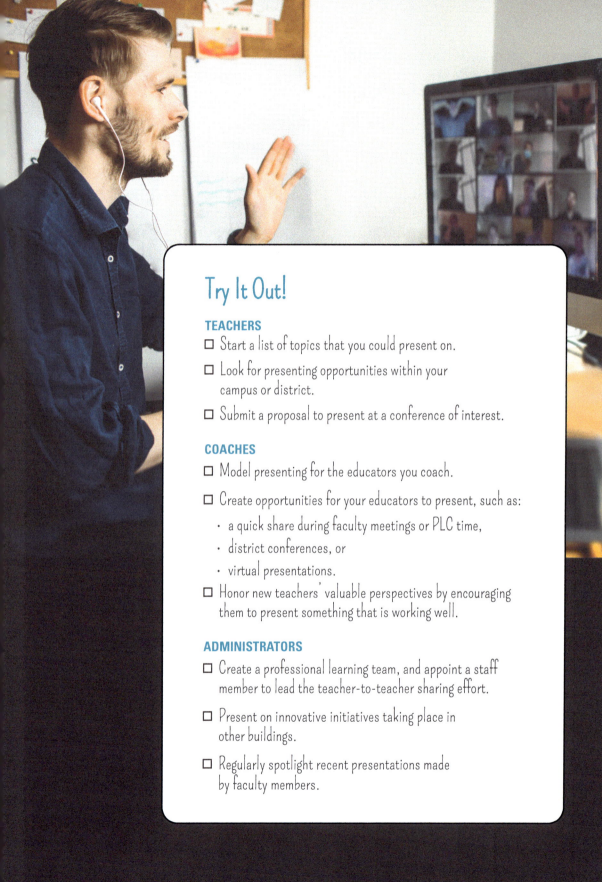

Try It Out!

TEACHERS
- ☐ Start a list of topics that you could present on.
- ☐ Look for presenting opportunities within your campus or district.
- ☐ Submit a proposal to present at a conference of interest.

COACHES
- ☐ Model presenting for the educators you coach.
- ☐ Create opportunities for your educators to present, such as:
  - a quick share during faculty meetings or PLC time,
  - district conferences, or
  - virtual presentations.
- ☐ Honor new teachers' valuable perspectives by encouraging them to present something that is working well.

ADMINISTRATORS
- ☐ Create a professional learning team, and appoint a staff member to lead the teacher-to-teacher sharing effort.
- ☐ Present on innovative initiatives taking place in other buildings.
- ☐ Regularly spotlight recent presentations made by faculty members.

Aspects to consider while reflecting on your learning.

DIRECTIONS
1. Choose a professional learning activity.
2. Evaluate that activity through the lens of each of these five aspects.
3. Mark on each line where the activity falls on the scale.

| Assigned learning activities | CHOICE | Self-selected learning activities |

| One-time learning experiences | CONTINUITY | Scheduled experiences throughout the year |

| Learning by yourself | COMMUNITY | Learning with colleagues |

| Learning about topics beyond your immediate need or context | CONNECTEDNESS | Learning about topics relevant to your context |

| Expensive | COST | Free |

REFLECT

- **Jot down** potential writing topics, graphics, or presentation ideas. What patterns do you notice in this list of ideas?
- **Describe** how job-embedded writing can enhance your instructional practice.
- **Explain** how creating a graphic of some sort would serve you professionally.
- **Evaluate** how presenting to colleagues would positively affect your practice.

©Seidlitz Education. All rights reserved.

4

"If 25% of your class can accomplish a task, then your entire class can accomplish that task through collaboration and cooperation."

Dr. Leo Gomez,
Gomez & Gomez Dual Language
Enrichment Model

INTERACTIVE PROFESSIONAL LEARNING

Carol's Journey

Learning is enhanced and accelerated when students connect, engage, and collaborate with others. Imagine that you walk into a classroom that is alive with activity. All students, regardless of their home languages or cultural backgrounds, are interacting with their environment, with each other, and with the content. The atmosphere is low stress, and the children seem to be directing their own learning.

Now imagine that type of professional learning and the impact it can have on educators. Guess what? This type of learning is available to you right now! Any time of day, you can join a community of professionals who are collaborating and sharing what they know about serving multilingual learners. Some of these peers may be in your building, and some may be on the other side of the world. Now more than ever, you can build a network of professionals with different levels of knowledge, different areas of expertise, and different perspectives that can all add value to your professional journey. This is your "professional learning network," or your PLN!

I remember being terrified for much of my first year as a classroom teacher, but I also had some major successes that year. I knew then — and I still know now — that those successes were the result of my interactions and collaborations with other teachers in the field. I learned early on that help will come spilling into your life if you just humble yourself enough to admit what you don't know. I knew that I was benefiting from my interactions with others, but I didn't realize that I was starting to build my own PLN.

As we said in earlier chapters, effective professional learning does not always need to be interactive. But we challenge you to consider the positive outcomes that are possible with interactive learning. When you open yourself up to collaboration with others, your learning becomes personalized as you voice your own questions, contribute ideas from your own background and experiences, and reflect on your own reality. These opportunities expand our learning potential beyond independent activities, and they empower us to better serve multilingual learners.

With the right network, we can feel comfortable taking risks. Those risks lead to more learning, and that learning leads to more growth — both for ourselves and for everyone in our networks!

Within his descriptions of the habits of highly effective people, Stephen Covey (2020) discusses a maturity continuum in which people shift from a dependence on others for the fulfillment of personal needs to an interdependence with others that values combining efforts to achieve greater success. That continuum is modeled in this book as it shifts its focus from professional learning in the context of a personal journey to collaborative learning that enhances and deepens individual learning through connection and engagement with others in the field. In these sections, we encourage you to go beyond the individual, personal, or local connections in order to develop relationships that best support your multilingual learners and fellow educators.

The education field is brimming with research establishing the benefits of interactive teaching methods. Interactive learning experiences have been shown to improve attendance, increase engagement, and boost learning outcomes (Deslauriers et al., 2011). While the teacher may be the best person to introduce new information to the class, researchers are advising that we reduce the amount of talking we do to encourage more interaction from students and, in turn, create better outcomes (Gewertz, 2019). Structured student to student interaction has been shown to have a positive effect on learning. Cooperative learning structures that include positive interdependence and individual accountability have a greater than average impact on student achievement. Studies consistently show students having percentile gains of approximately 19 points (effect size = .43) when teachers facilitate structured student to student interaction (Dean et al., 2012).

These same interactive learning principles can also introduce powerful benefits to our own professional learning. If interactive learning results in academic gains for students by requiring them to apply new information instead of merely taking note of it, it stands to reason that the same processes will enhance educators' acquisition of knowledge and professional growth as well. In other words, firsthand use of new material develops personal ownership for students and teachers.

Earlier in this text, the case was made for the benefits of interpretive professional learning and expressive professional learning. It might be helpful to refer back to those sections, review their substantial benefits, and then consider that interactive learning offers the best of both worlds, with an ebb and flow that is controlled by the learner.

INTERACTIVE LEARNING IS	INTERACTIVE LEARNING IS NOT
- engaging - active - both receiving new ideas and contributing from your own background and experiences - an opportunity to construct new knowledge through exploring, questioning, and problem solving - an opportunity for participants to be honored for the unique perspectives and backgrounds that they all bring - something that can be done anonymously	- something that must always be done publicly - something that must be done continuously - something that must be time consuming - only for "experts" in the field

CONNECT

It is common for teachers to work in isolation from their colleagues (Calderón et al., 2019), and this is especially true for language acquisition specialists, who are sometimes the only one in their building (or perhaps even the only one across multiple schools or sites). While content teachers and grade-level teachers have teams with which to collaborate, that is not always the case for teachers who focus on language acquisition. This can lead to a sense of disconnectedness, and our jobs can start to feel lonely.

In her compelling book detailing how brain science influences learning, Hammond (2015) references our "social engagement system" (p.44), which compels us to be connected with others in the community. Essentially, our brains are hardwired to seek out connections and positive relationships because "the brain needs to be part of a caring social community to maximize its sense of well-being" (p.47). This desire to connect likely resonates with many teachers, which can make a lack of connectedness at work feel especially frustrating. Research shows that educators in strong collaborative environments see significant benefits in their practices (Cohan et al., 2019), but many teachers are still planning, teaching, and examining their practices alone (Mirel & Goldin, 2012). This does not have to be the case for you! You can capitalize on the benefits of community by seeking out connections from a variety of sources. While our networks can certainly benefit from the perspectives of students, community members, and parents, this chapter focuses on building a network of professional colleagues who share a focus on supporting multilingual learners.

As you begin to connect with other educators, some individuals will serve as temporary companions on your learning journey, while others will become foundational members of your professional learning network and will travel with you for years to come. With our networks now composed of a significant number of digital connections, Whitby (2013) affirms that a PLN, when used actively, can be a tool to support our personal and professional growth in ways that were not possible before. In general, PLNs can capitalize on social media and technology to eliminate the barriers of time and space so educators can communicate, collaborate, create, and reflect with connected colleagues.

Where can we teachers make and foster these digital connections? While there are certainly online forums and message boards for educators, the most useful channel is often simply social media – and, in particular, Twitter – where teachers from all over the world can connect and converse any time and at no cost. In addition to being far-reaching in terms of membership, social media platforms provide a large variety of ways in which people can connect, chat, ask questions, request information, and collectively investigate educational issues, problems, and solutions.

Professional Colleagues

SEEKING OUT PROFESSIONAL COLLEAGUES

As you start to grow your network, determine which colleagues are a good fit for your needs by prioritizing your learning goals and narrowing your focus to short-term objectives and long-range targets. For example, you may want to improve several aspects of your whole-group instruction to make content more comprehensible, but classroom management is your highest priority. Start by seeking out a colleague with proven classroom management skills. Factors such as content area, grade level, personality, and willingness to collaborate will guide you toward the best colleague connections. In the event that you do not have anyone at your school with expertise in a specific area of need, you might broaden your lens to consider the gifts that every person brings. You may also want to adjust your plan to include collaborating with a new or novice educator. Just as veteran teachers bring valuable insight from years of experience, our newest professionals bring fresh eyes that can offer a novel perspective on established teaching practices.

CONNECTING WITH PROFESSIONAL COLLEAGUES

Opportunities to gather with colleagues, such as at staff and committee meetings, can be a way to connect and learn in community; however, these occasions do not necessarily afford us the choice and flexibility to focus on the content we find most valuable in serving students who are acquiring a target language. The emphasis here is on voluntary, personalized connections – online or off – that focus on professional learning in shared areas of particular interest or need. Keeping our sights on our goal of supporting self-directed professional learning, we suggest you connect with others. Sharing resources informally and reflecting about their value and applicability can be done through:

- Actively engaging in professional learning workshops/learning labs
- Participating in "learning walks"
- Attending and contributing to unconferences

Katie's Journey

Something super simple I started doing with a teacher friend that fosters connection is a "daily plus" text exchange. Every day, we send each other a text detailing one positive thing that happened at work. It's a simple routine that helps us reflect on what is going well for us, focus on positivity, and stay connected. Sometimes when we read each other's texts, we simply celebrate and reply with something like "yay" or "that's awesome." Other times, like when my friend mentioned a morning meeting lesson that went really well, my response was, "Tell me more!" This quick text exchange is a great way to be aware of all the things that make a colleague feel successful and to get perspective about what they are doing in their classrooms.

ACTIVELY ENGAGING IN PROFESSIONAL LEARNING WORKSHOPS/LEARNING LABS

PARTICIPATING IN "LEARNING WALKS"

ATTENDING AND CONTRIBUTING TO UNCONFERENCES

for Educators of Multilingual Learners

Experts in the Field

SEEKING OUT EXPERTS IN THE FIELD

In his book, *Who Owns the Learning*, Alan November challenges our thinking about what is available to learners and reminds us that, through technology, we have power beyond what we could have imagined just a few years ago (2012). We are no longer restricted by the learning we can find in our own geographic locations. Not only can we learn with others around the world, but we can also interact with experts in the field. This may have once seemed like an opportunity only afforded to educators with the largest budgets for professional development, but that is no longer the case. In a connected world, these opportunities exist for free, and many educators are able to take advantage of them just by inquiring.

To determine which experts are a good fit for your learning journey, consider some of the instructional skills necessary for supporting multilingual learners. You will find that there are experts in areas such as co-teaching, culturally responsive teaching, and dedicated instructional practices for early childhood education, secondary classrooms, and newcomers, among others.

Once you have a focus area, it becomes easier to seek out the experts who will add the most value to your journey. Taking stock of priorities for your own professional growth is the best place to start. Being a connected educator is your best bet for finding experts who are willing to interact with you and your colleagues, as interacting in various learning communities will shed light on the experts who are actively engaging with others in webinars, Twitter chats, and book studies.

CONNECTING WITH EXPERTS IN THE FIELD

The idea of interacting with an expert can seem intimidating; however, it's important to remember that experts in the field are very passionate about their work and areas of focus. Many empathize with our challenges as teachers of culturally and linguistically diverse students and share our excitement for supporting these students. Here are some ideas for ways to connect with an expert in your area of interest:

- Send an email to express appreciation for their work. Share what you've learned from them and how it has made a difference in your teaching.
- Engage with their content on social networking platforms by commenting, sharing, and asking questions.
- Tweet about the professional book you're reading, and tag the author.
- Invite an author to join in a virtual meeting after you have studied their book.
- Ask an expert to guest moderate a Twitter chat around their topic of expertise.
- Interview an expert for a blog post, podcast, or article highlighting their work.

There's always the possibility that your efforts will not result in a return correspondence from an expert. Bear in mind, the people you're reaching out to are likely very busy and some may be new to various social networking platforms. However, the potential to make a positive connection is still very strong.

Katie's Journey

When we were reading Carol's book, *Boosting Achievement*, for #MLLChat_BkClub, I tagged Jana Echevarria in the following tweet.

Katie Toppel, Ed.D.
@Toppel_ELD

Replying to @Jechev and @Seidlitz_Ed

@Jechev We'd love to have you join our #ELLChat_BkClub slow chat!

9:13 PM · Jul 8, 2017 · Twitter for iPhone

Jana Echevarria, PhD @Jechev · Sep 21, 2017
Replying to @Toppel_ELD
I really appreciate all the great ideas and feedback about the book. Keep it coming! :) We're a community with a common cause.

♡ 1   ⇅   ♡ 4   ⬆

Not only did she reply, but she also started participating in our PLN chats and both she and her co-author, Julie Nora, engaged with us when we read their book, *No More Low Expectations for English Learners*. As if that wasn't enough, when we invited the authors to participate in a live virtual meeting with some of us who had read the book, Jana joined us from Spain! Having the author herself participate in our book club and share insights with our readers was an opportunity many of our readers had never thought possible, and more importantly, it was a fabulous way to enhance our learning.

Professional Conferences

CONNECTING AT PROFESSIONAL CONFERENCES

Conferences are a great platform for interacting with both experts who share your areas of interest and educators of multilingual learners. Meals, breaks, and social time are often built into the schedule to provide windows of time for connecting with colleagues. Some conferences even have designated times and locations specifically for networking, where you can feel confident that everyone present shares the intention of meeting and talking to virtual strangers. Here are some additional suggestions for connecting at conferences:

- Sit next to a person or group you don't know during a session, or ask them to join you for lunch.
- Be on the lookout for people who are sitting alone. Not all people attend conferences in groups, and they might appreciate a conference buddy.
- Preview the conference schedule and choose which sessions you plan to attend. Reach out to session presenters ahead of time via email to let them know you are interested in their work and plan to be in their session.
- Introduce yourself. We can all relate to feeling intimidated by presenters – particularly if they are well known – but as presenters, we always appreciate it when people come to talk to us.
- Bring business cards, and share them widely.
- Reach out after the conference to presenters whose sessions you enjoyed. Tell them what you liked or your biggest takeaways. Ask questions, and offer them more insight.

Try It Out!

TEACHERS
- ☐ Brainstorm and rank your professional learning goals.
- ☐ Determine where to begin your search for people who will support your professional learning.
- ☐ Introduce yourself to a new professional connection.

COACHES
- ☐ Leverage social media to find other instructional coaches.
- ☐ Take business cards to conferences with the intention of growing your network.
- ☐ Help teachers facilitate connections with each other.

ADMINISTRATORS
- ☐ Participate in a social media chat for administrators.
- ☐ Actively seek out other administrators to widen your learning network.
- ☐ Prioritize and protect time for faculty to connect and collaborate.

ENGAGE

Long before the idea of a PLN was commonly known, foundational scholars in our field recognized the importance of social learning (Bandura, 1977; Williams, 1989). They drew attention to the significant role language plays in learning, because "talk gives us the opportunity to organize our thinking into coherent utterances, hear how our thinking sounds out loud, listen to how others respond, and often, hear others add to or expand on our thinking" (Hammond, 2015, p.134). When we learn on our own, we may not invest sufficient time to reflect or think about what we've learned (Hammond, 2015). However, in the context of a conversation, we exchange our thoughts, perspectives, and reflections with others, which can result in a deeper, more nuanced comprehension of the subject matter (Fisher et al., 2008). Consequently, cooperative learning has remained a longstanding staple in classrooms because opportunities to work and learn with peers positively influences student achievement (Johnson & Johnson, 2009; Kagan, 2010; Slavin, 1991).

The interpretive and expressive pathways for learning represent a multitude of productive and valuable opportunities for increasing your knowledge base as well as your second language acquisition instructional skills. That knowledge and those skills can be useful when engaging in learning with and from others. Once you have sought out and connected with some new professional allies, the next step is to activate the benefits of social learning by sharing, revising, refining, and elevating your professional knowledge in the company of other dedicated colleagues. Chapters 2 and 3 featured many different options for independent learning, this section will build on those ideas and provide suggestions for transforming interpretive and expressive learning paths into interactive ones. As you read, listen, watch, write, create, or present, you process the information through your personal worldview (Hammond, 2015). Your experiences, instructional context, cultural values, and biases will all influence

the mindset through which you filter what you're learning.

One of the distinct benefits of such socially constructed learning is the access to multiple perspectives. Rather than approaching a topic, issue, or problem with a singular viewpoint, you can elicit ideas from other language learning professionals who come with a variety of experiences, backgrounds, and perspectives. Years of equity training have taught us that "we don't know what we don't know," which reinforces the need to collectively construct knowledge so that we don't inadvertently marginalize the voices and experiences of certain populations in our teaching. We need each other. Our learning, depth of understanding, and ability to effectively serve diverse populations of students depend on our ability to approach professional learning endeavors in solidarity.

SYNCHRONOUS & ASYNCHRONOUS INTERACTIONS

As we strive to make learning more interactive, both synchronous and asynchronous interactions need to be considered since each type of communication is valuable for different reasons. Synchronous interactions offer opportunities to interact in real time and can provide a more natural flow of conversation, which sets the stage for quicker feedback and response rates. Twitter chats are an example of synchronous interactive learning, as participants come together at recurring times for synchronized live chats around particular topics. This option may preclude certain individuals from participating if they're unavailable at the time of the chat, but they are wonderful opportunities for those who can participate.

Asynchronous communication offers the ability to contribute to a dialogue or conversation on our own time and then check back in later to see what others have said. Because this option provides more flexibility in terms of time commitment, it opens the door for participation from broader groups. Another benefit of asynchronous learning opportunities is that they level the playing field in terms of background, subject matter knowledge, and access to technology. We can take more time to comprehend, research, and then craft meaningful contributions when we have time and access to the platform.

For example, since we collaborated on this book project from three different time zones (Pacific Standard, Central Standard, and Indochina), we used an app that allowed us to leave voice recordings in a group chat so that we could share ideas as we were each working so the others could listen and respond at a time that was convenient. We also used video chats to meet synchronously when we needed to have live conversations about revising our writing so we could accomplish a more substantial amount of work.

> Asynchronous communication offers the ability to contribute to a dialogue or conversation on our own time and then check back in later to see what others have said.

From Independent to Interactive Reading

While reading professional texts, there are many ways to experience deeper learning through conversation. These discussions provide a platform to talk about content, exchange ideas, answer questions, and apply the information specifically to your personal or collective context. Group members benefit because reciprocal sharing adds additional layers of learning and reflection. Ideas are built up collectively through conversations, so you can walk away with insights or perspectives you may not have initially had when you read on your own (Zwiers, 2019). Also, as you read independently with the intention to interact, you may engage in deeper thinking as you prepare to share your thoughts and takeaways with the group.

DOING A BOOK STUDY

A book study is a great way to organize discussions around a particular book that a group of people read together. When a book study is done as part of district or building-level professional learning, there is likely a designated leader who provides particular reflection questions to foster collective thought around the book's content as it applies to the group's particular context (i.e., school initiatives, adopted curricula, targeted areas of growth). In this case, participants might have a structured reading schedule and regular meetings. However, if it is being done outside of school, there can be a lot of flexibility in the format, formality, and frequency of a book study so that it can meet a variety of needs and preferences. For example, members may decide to convene in more social contexts, but still with a specific focus on discussing the book's content. This type of book study may come about more authentically when educators take an interest in a particular topic. Fortunately, you can mold a book study in the way that best supports your learning and share in that learning with other eager participants.

DOING A VIRTUAL BOOK STUDY

Though book studies traditionally take place in person, they can also be done online. A virtual book study can have the same structure and benefits as an in-person book study, but the doors are opened for participants from various locations and contexts to share in the learning. Virtual book studies can use a variety of digital platforms to provide time and space for participants to synchronously or asynchronously share what they have learned, their favorite parts, and responses to questions. Social media groups and networks both provide opportunities to seek out other professionals with shared interests who might want to participate in a virtual book study. Groups can arrange to do virtual meetups or simply provide a particular digital space where participants can post about what they are learning.

Replying to @KatieToppel @LeticiaTrower and @COSALeaders

#ELLChat_BkClub has not only helped me stay up to date professionally, it has given me the courage and support to try new practices and strategies. It's given me an instructional sounding board to inspire me - and the ability to interact with authors! Plus life-long #pln friends!

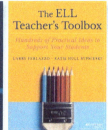

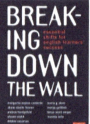
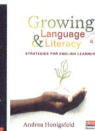
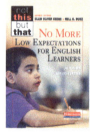
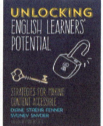

#MLLChat_BkClub (formerly #ELLChat_BkClub) is an example of a virtual book club that operates via Twitter as a slow chat for asynchronous engagement. A professional learning network of educators from across the globe have come together to form a community committed to improving instruction for multilingual learners through continuous personal learning. Participants access quality professional development that honors the need for choice and flexibility. For each round, participants can:

- take part in selecting/voting on books to read;
- access a suggested reading timeline;
- post reactions, thoughts, favorite quotes, BookSnaps, highlighted text, etc.; and
- respond to weekly questions to engage in reflection and dialogue.

Dr. C. Tennyson
@CBTennyson

Replying to @missnoravaldez @MsSalvac and 8 others

I feel the exact same way. My personal/professional growth has skyrocketed since I joined #Ellchat_BkClub Thanks @Toppel_ELD and @TanELLclassroom for giving a marginalized group of Ts a voice and platform for learning from each other!

7:50 PM · Apr 18, 2018 from Tennessee, USA · Twitter for iPhone

POSTING IN DIGITAL PLATFORMS

If a formal book study is not the best fit, there are other ways to interact that come with even greater flexibility, such as posting about what you're reading on a variety of social media platforms. Take note of trending hashtags in groups that are sharing information for supporting multilingual learners. Join the discussions currently happening within these groups by finding materials (graphics, sketchnotes, articles, post discussions, etc.) that have been posted by other members that are relevant to you and commenting with your own insights or experiences.

Creating graphics is another way to interact with others on material you've covered independently. It is one of the ways to show what you have learned in a format that is enticing and gives context to other people who may or may not have read the same text. BookSnaps, sketchnotes, and infographics (see pgs. 55-61) are all visual ways to share what you like and want to remember from texts. When you create and share these images, you are inviting other people to share in your learning, which creates space for interaction. One thing to keep in mind when creating and sharing graphics is the importance of citing the source. Make sure to clearly identify the text and author(s) so viewers know where the quotes or ideas come from.

Below is a book snap I created while reading Dr. Michelle Yzquierdo's book, Pathways to Greatness. *I create these BookSnaps to help me process the content. As I share them on social media, some produce a discussion among other book club readers, and the discussion can further my learning.* **– Tan**

Cooperative learning is especially beneficial to newcomers because it not only helps the development of language, but it also **helps the learning of content concepts in a structured, safe, and non threatening way.**

INVITING THE AUTHOR

Many authors connect with schools that are doing book studies on their work around serving diverse populations. Educators can ask specific questions, and the author gets to connect with the people who are using the work authentically with different groups of students. If this is of interest to you, reach out to an author to see if they are open to scheduling a video conference with your book study group. This type of opportunity opens up interactive possibilities for your team prior to, during, and after the call. If you tag authors in your posts in virtual settings, they may comment back, which gives you another opportunity to engage in conversation or get their feedback.

After reading independently, we hope you'll try some of these ideas for making your reading experiences interactive in order to broaden your learning by learning with others.

for Educators of Multilingual Learners

From Independent to Interactive Watching

As we all know, watching another person teach something or explain a concept is a foundational part of learning. This act of receiving information is important on its own, but turning that into an interactive experience can make it even more powerful. With so much research on the benefits of interactive learning (see p.68), here are a few examples of how to turn a watching activity (e.g., viewing a webinar) into an interactive professional learning experience.

CHATTING WITH OTHERS IN THE EVENT

Events like webinars are streamed in real time over the internet and are meant to be viewed by large audiences. With so many viewers, opportunities to interact with the presenter may consist of submitting questions ahead of time or responding to poll questions during the event. While this limited interaction can be useful, there are other ways to engage since the presenter is not the only source of knowledge in any room. The chat function of a live stream offers a way for viewers to interact with each other during the presentation. Interacting with like-minded professionals may be especially meaningful to educators who are the only language teachers in their teams or schools. By participating in the chat, you can pose your own questions, respond to fellow viewers, and expand your learning by discussing the content with others as it is presented.

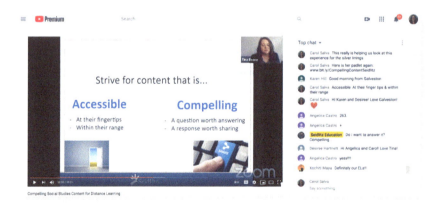

CHATTING WITH OTHERS ON SOCIAL MEDIA

Consider leveraging your network as much as possible. Your PLN can turn any event into an interactive experience. In fact, sharing knowledge with your PLN is at the heart of the information revolution, according to technology philosopher David Weinberger (2014), and as discussed on p. 63. As we share information beyond our small circles, our networks have the potential to become more knowledgeable than any presenter or any group of individuals in a particular session. Armed with this understanding, we challenge you to share what you are learning on social media platforms. If you think the content is worth sharing, you can post the most valuable takeaways as you watch to capture the essential ideas. If other members of your PLN are watching an event about serving multilingual learners at the same time, live-posting is a great way to engage in conversation with an audience to whom you are more connected (as opposed to the entire audience viewing the webinar). Using event hashtags, posting to specific groups, or tagging key people is a way to interact with our PLNs and draw from their experiences as we build our collective strength and knowledge around serving diverse learners.

WATCH PARTIES

Even though webinars are accessible for individuals to view on their own, it doesn't mean we need to watch them in isolation. Consider gathering your colleagues or members of your PLN to watch the event together. This can happen in a physical space like a classroom or a conference room, but it can also happen remotely with everyone watching from their own home while linked together virtually. Conferencing software can allow one member to share their screen so that your small group can be chatting together about the event with the intention of sharing comments on how the learning affects your group's needs. Scheduling time to talk before and after the event is also a great way to engage and expand on the learning.

USING THE CONTENT IN REPLAY

When presenters make replays available of their live events, this offers tremendous potential to utilize the content after the session is over. Capitalizing on the collaborative nature of a watch party, a synchronous learning session can be scheduled for any time that is convenient for the group. This type of activity calls for even more interaction by allowing viewers to stop and start the video for note taking, reflection, or processing.

From Independent to Interactive Writing

In Chapter 3, we discussed the value of writing as a way to reflect on our experiences and foster professional growth. Writing is a personal process of expressing our thinking in ways that solidify our ideas. In some cases, writing is entirely individual, yet in other circumstances, as with blogging, writing is shared publicly and becomes an opportunity for interactive learning.

BLOGS

The audience can interact with the blogger by validating or even sometimes challenging their ideas or practices, which can turn individual writing into a rich opportunity for discussion and growth. Additionally, readers can contribute alternative ideas not mentioned by the blogger. Boland and Tenkasi (2004) call this professional interaction perspective making and perspective taking. Perspective making is when we write to establish viewpoints while perspective taking is adopting the readers' interpretations. Maintaining a professional blog provides you with the opportunity to add to readers' perspectives while they add to your perspective through their comments on the blog, the emails they send you, and their comments on social media posts. This perspective-expanding experience is an example of valuable professional learning.

Tan's Journey

One of my most-viewed tweets was one where I shared an article about the types of scaffolding for multilingual learners. I've revised the original blog article based on some of the feedback I received via that tweet and other sources. Halla Jmourko reminded me that there are two additional types of scaffolds that I had forgotten to include: linguistic and environmental (2018). Additionally, I had originally connected each of the scaffolding types to a learning style, but Emma Gore-Lloyd tweeted a response pointing out that the concept of learning styles is not empirically valid. She even provided a link to a research article about the topic. I then updated my article and the accompanying infographic to incorporate their feedback. This is an example of how blogging for a public audience grows and expands the blogger's understanding.

Halla Jmourko
@HallaJmourko

Replying to @TanKHuynh

I'd to share a tool I developed emphasizing the need of situating #scaffolding #LD Supports in #LearningEnvironment inclusive of diversity. #ELLs who engage when supported in comprehension of & communication during lessons. #LD Supports are extended to include Verbal & Textual.

82 DIY PD: A Guide to Self-Directed Learning

Katie's Journey

When I started out as a blogger, I don't think anyone even read what I was writing. However, as time went on, I did gain some followers, and I knew this because people started leaving comments. It was always so exciting to get a notification that someone had left a comment, because it was a chance to get additional insight on the topics I had written about. I started incorporating questions at the end of each post as a way to encourage people to add to the conversation, and I found that this made people more likely to comment on posts because the questions served as an invitation for them to share their own thinking. Rather than saying something generic like "great post," they would leave more detailed responses that specifically addressed the theme of the post. Posing questions allowed me and other readers to access different perspectives and contexts related to my content.

You can also make blogging interactive by writing about current events that impact your professional circle. Take, for example, school closures due to the COVID-19 pandemic. Many bloggers used their platforms to interact with teachers to provide timely advice, share suggestions, offer different perspectives, and make their own closure navigation experiences public. The quick insights, coupled with the boosted feelings of solidarity, made these blogs great resources throughout the pandemic.

In addition, as a blogger, you can actively interact with your readers by asking them to contribute to your blog. For example, if you are blogging about multilingual learners at the secondary level, you might ask an educator who works in elementary schools to write a guest post. This adds value to your blog, and it also grows your practice. Through this interaction, you can simultaneously maintain your blog while learning from your guest blogger.

The final and most important distinction of running a blog as compared to maintaining a private education journal is the sustained

professional reflection. If you amass an audience, your interaction with the readers will motivate and supercharge you to continue reflecting, to create more resources, to research more, and to share with a wider community. As you give to a community through blogging, your audience will refine and challenge your knowledge by shedding light on alternative perspectives that will evolve your practice. In blogging, learning is a two-way street.

Carol's Journey

When I first began blogging, the statistics on my blog indicated that no one was really reading it. I was a bit disappointed that there was no interaction, but I have always tried to write as part of my learning journey, so I just kept blogging.

Nowadays, I prefer to reflect about my learning in the form of a podcast. I'm still adding to the blog, but most of the posts are actually show notes. The act of writing up the notes has turned out to be a great way to get even more reflection down in writing. While it did not start out as an interactive blog, I am now getting quite a bit of feedback on these entries. Some of that interaction happens in the comment section of the blog, and some happens on social media where I am sharing posts. I appreciate the questions, the insight, and the suggestions I get from readers and listeners. As I share more, I get more. The blog is just another example of how my PLN truly shapes how I am thinking, what I am sharing, and the direction of my learning.

Try It Out!

TEACHERS
- ☐ Join or start a professional book study.
- ☐ Invite an expert in the field to video conference with your team after a book study of their work.
- ☐ Share a blog post you've written with your professional learning network and request feedback.

COACHES
- ☐ Facilitate a podcast listening party, and pause periodically to allow for conversation.
- ☐ Model interactive learning experiences for the faculty.
- ☐ Organize and lead a social media chat, book study, or watch party.

ADMINISTRATORS
- ☐ Model interactive learning with other administrators.
- ☐ Schedule time for interactive learning experiences.
- ☐ Highlight examples of interactive learning in your learning community.

COLLABORATE

Connecting with and engaging with other language professionals in the field moves us away from isolation and toward collaborative practices that enhance our skills and our efficacy in our roles. Collaboration offers us opportunities to work together for a variety of purposes. The practice of professional collaboration is a way for teachers to:
- combine expertise,
- nurture new and creative ideas,
- make task completion more efficient and effective,
- get feedback on processes and outcomes,
- experience enhanced motivation, and
- create opportunities for reflection. (Cohan et al., 2019).

Collaborating with colleagues offers many benefits and can come to fruition in many different ways and in many different contexts. However, unlike simply connecting, collaborating also implies action. Collaboration takes place when professionals come together for a shared purpose or work together toward a particular outcome. The benefits of collaboration are far-reaching and encompass positive outcomes for a variety of stake-holders, including teachers, families, and students.

Co-Create

In Chapter 3, we shared different ways you can learn through the process of creating. In this section, our focus shifts to creating collaboratively, which brings the opportunity to pool your best skills and talents with others in a team effort. Maybe you have great ideas but lack the technology skills to make a project come to life. Or maybe you have expertise in teaching language but want to make sure your project accurately reflects content standards and expectations. Teaming up with a partner or a group whose strengths complement your own is a great way to produce a product that represents collective knowledge. Any time there is an opportunity to put heads together (especially when contributors represent different

lenses, roles, demographics, or skill sets), the outcome is surely enhanced.

The opportunities to learn from co-created projects are twofold. The educators who engage in the collaborative creation process benefit from working with and learning from one another. Also, the educators who access the new content benefit from the collective wisdom being shared. Working in partnership with others involves giving and receiving feedback, which can contribute to refinement and clarity in your professional knowledge, beliefs, and assertions. You may have dialogue with your co-creators around what information should and should not be included or how to best convey ideas in a succinct, clear format. If your group members represent expertise in different areas, you may also find yourself learning a lot from your teammates as a result of their unique contributions. These interactions among team members show us that even if your goal is to create something that will support other educators in their learning, you and your teammates are still likely to benefit as a result of the creation process.

CO-CREATING GRAPHICS

Collaborating to create graphics is a way to combine professional knowledge and technology innovation in a doubly meaningful learning opportunity for educators. When the creation process is shared, the audience will benefit from all the knowledge funneled through a wider spectrum of experience. Viewers may also gain insight into technology tools or digital formats they can use themselves, which may spark additional curiosity for professional learning.

ELL 2.0 is our passion project.

Each Tuesday at 4:00 p.m., we share a new resource for language educators on our website and Twitter. We have been collaborating on this work for more than two years and we have created numerous articles, tools, tutorials, videos, and infographics that have been used by teachers we coach, university students, and virtual colleagues from around the world.

Shory & McGarth, 2019

When we first began collaborating, we worked side by side at coffee shops or at work. We would brainstorm ideas, decide on the topic and resources, and then create a plan for completing our work. As we've gained experience as collaborators and our trust in each other has grown, we can now work asynchronously. We no longer have to have official brainstorming sessions. One of us will now start our creations in our ELL 2.0 Google Drive and ask the other to jump in and add her unique perspective or expertise. We go back and forth on a project, building on each other's ideas — which includes content and aesthetics — until we are both satisfied with the final result. At that point, usually after three or four rounds of edits, we post it to our site. It's hard to look at a project and see who did what because it's really a collaborative mixture of information, creativity, and personal experience.

Some of the benefits of collaboration include learning from each other, discussing new ideas in a safe space, being vulnerable enough to ask for support in certain areas, using our unique expertise to support the project, and keeping each other accountable for a weekly deadline. Publishing each week changes the way we read, learn, and interact with colleagues and students because we are now always on alert for good things to build and share in order to support educators and students.

Michelle Makus Shory
ESL Instruction Coach, ELL2.0

Irina McGarth PhD
Education Recovery & Literacy Specialist, ELL2.0

CO-WRITING

Writing collaboratively ensures that content is filtered through more than one viewpoint before it is shared with others. Co-authors can include their unique perspectives based on how their roles, contexts, and experiences apply to the focus of the text. Co-authors can also increase clarity in their shared writing by asking each other to elaborate, give examples, or to make their writing more succinct when necessary. Hearing how someone else interprets your writing can definitely help pinpoint areas that could benefit from revision or elaboration if the message is not coming across as intended. Collaborative writing also comes with built-in editors, because teams can review each other's contributions with fresh eyes to avoid publishing anything that contains errors or potential misinformation.

Even if you write a piece on your own, sharing it with trusted colleagues to review before you share it publicly may elicit perspectives or suggestions that you had not initially considered. This is another form of collaboration because it reflects a collective voice and results in enhanced learning for both the author(s) and the audience. Regardless of the process, there is a significant benefit in having more than one person contribute to writing that will be shared.

CO-CREATING VIDEOS

Educators who have the opportunity to see instructional practices with a wider lens can be a valuable resource for locating the ideal footage that will best support teachers in their areas of interest or need. Instructional coaches, teachers on special assignment, and administrators are in the unique position of observing a wide variety of teachers and teaching practices as part of their work. Educators in these roles can support teachers by capturing, curating, and circulating video footage of effective practices being modeled with students. This process

---

Truthfully, when we started our blog two years ago, we didn't really know why we were doing it. Blogging just seemed like a fun way to record our experiences co-teaching together (and it is!), but we quickly learned co-authoring a blog has real benefits that have made us better co-teachers.

Co-blogging challenges us to be creative and refine our voice as a team, and it pushes us to be positive and seek out our successes. There is a very real pressure with a blog to ensure that all aspects are done well. Our goal is to make our posts as engaging and informative as possible. To foster collective ownership, we always give each other the opportunity to edit and review all posts prior to publishing them on our site. Our co-authoring dynamic also further develops that sense of trust needed to be successful co-teachers.

It empowers us to share our journey, connect with other educators, and advocate for inclusion. Learning from others is one of the major benefits of blogging. It's also a great form of co-reflection. We learn more from reflecting on our experiences than from the experiences themselves, and co-authoring a blog is the best thinking activity! It forces us to think critically about our teaching and learning, and then organize our ideas to share.

It's also a way to sharpen our collaborative skills. Like any skill, the more you practice collaborating, the better you get. Sharing a blog gives us the opportunity to collaborate, problem solve, agree or compromise, and make decisions together outside the classroom, which only increases our collaborative strength inside the classroom.

Allyson Caudill, John Cox, Ashley Blackley
Classroom Teachers & Bloggers at
"Ready, Set, Coteach!"

becomes more collaborative as teachers who are willing to be filmed become more involved in the creation process.

To enhance the learning value, these kinds of videos can contain prompts that ask viewers to pause the video and reflect on a particular part of the recorded lesson. Instructional coaches can also provide commentary after the prompts to provide more perspective on the value of featured second language acquisition instructional tools or strategies.

As Tier 1 coaches, we each partner, collaborate, and co-teach with over 80 teachers to implement classroom management strategies that support the social-emotional well-being of our students. As partners in classrooms, we are fortunate to have a unique perspective on working with a variety of kindergarten through fifth grade classes each week. This allows us to see the amazing work students and teachers are doing on a daily basis. We capture video clips that showcase teachers modeling strategies and ideas so other teachers can benefit from seeing them in action in real classrooms. We each cover a different grade band, so we work together to create compilation videos that highlight best practices across grade levels and schools. Our intention in creating videos is to support teachers, but we have also become more tech savvy in the process of learning how to create the videos that convey information in a fun and engaging way.

Sheri LeDrew, Colleen Thompson, and Aimee Biggs
Tier 1 Positive Behavior Support Coaches, Tigard Tualatin School District

Co-Facilitate

Whether you are going to facilitate a lesson on characterization, a webinar on family engagement, or a workshop on sheltered instruction, you can enhance your own professional learning even further by thinking through several specific activities before, during, and after your content is delivered.

Co-teachers are not the only professionals who have the advantages of collaboration available to them. Co-facilitators can also experience these benefits. Our experiences with delivering professional learning sessions in partnership with colleagues have provided opportunities for collaboration that are very similar to co-teaching. We encourage you to consider the parallels between the professional learning benefits of co-teaching students and the professional learning benefits of co-facilitating adult learning experiences.

GETTING STARTED
When thinking about where to start with co-facilitating, we suggest aligning your goals to best practices of co-teaching. For example, Cohan, Honigsfeld, and Dove (2019) offer that effective collaboration among educators includes the following elements:

- Targeted discussions
- Data analysis
- Standards reviews
- Co-construction of essential curricula
- Lesson planning
- The development of assessment tools and techniques
- The thoughtful examination and re-examination of instruction delivery

Whether you are co-planning an after-school training or a virtual workshop for hundreds of viewers, it is important to think through best practices of good collaboration with your co-facilitator to ensure you are incorporating what makes sense for the best lesson delivery. Our own professional growth begins to expand when we each bring our own perspectives and knowledge to the planning, which affords us an opportunity to draw from our peers'.

FINDING THE RIGHT PARTNER

Should you be in a position to choose a co-facilitator, that search might stretch well beyond your physical space. The three of us have presented at many events together despite the fact that we live in three very different areas of the globe. Technology now offers many free conferencing options and digital workspaces to collaborate synchronously or asynchronously around a presentation. More important factors to consider may be traits such as personality, area of expertise, depth of knowledge, and other characteristics that complement your own. A colleague with a differing perspective may be ideal in that your skill sets can come together to enrich not only the presentation but also the other presenter's professional expertise. The same can be true of working with a colleague from another country or cultural background. Working with international partners can help us build understanding of different perspectives, adopt alternative approaches to learning, and it may enhance our interest in and knowledge of global issues (Salva & Matis, 2017).

REFLECTING TO GROW FURTHER

The end of a presentation can also be the beginning of more collective learning. During your presentation, you and your co-facilitator can be mindful about what you want to discuss in reflection. For example, because there are two of you, one of the facilitators can function as a surveyor, reading participants' reactions while the other is teaching. This offers specific talking points for post-presentation reflections. Another opportunity for professional growth in reflection is having another perspective as you review any feedback you receive from your audience. Because your co-facilitator is someone who has shared in the entire experience with you, they can celebrate effectiveness with you and also help you put critical feedback in perspective. Together you can help each other see areas for growth in positive and constructive ways.

RECOGNIZING CHALLENGES

Co-facilitating may be one of the most difficult things we take on as education professionals, but as with many things, the enhanced experience is worth the effort it requires. For example, the partnership between language teachers and content teachers is not an easy one for a variety of reasons, including the typical struggle of working with different personalities and different levels of readiness among professionals (Davison, 2006). Other collaborations may seem difficult because many of us are used to working in a culture of isolation (Calderón et al., 2019), and some of us may not be ready to make concessions on our educational point of view. Psychologist and educational leadership consultant Robert Evans points out that asking us to change our craft can be seen as a devaluation of what we have learned and even who we have been learning from – and that can be difficult to accept because we hold our teaching very close to our hearts (Schwartz, 2017).

So why do we recommend that you go to all the trouble? We recognize that facilitating with another person around serving multilingual learners can be a challenge, but our experiences have proven to be more rewarding than challenging, over and over again.

In 2018, Katie Toppel, Carlota Holder, and I collaborated remotely from different locations in the United States to prepare a presentation for the SIOP National Conference. We actually did not meet in person until we all arrived in Seattle for the conference, but we worked together both synchronously and asynchronously in the months leading up to the event in order to prepare. Although we could each have done individual presentations, we teamed up because, among the three of us, we represent elementary school, high school, and administration. Our collective experience with co-teaching using the SIOP model made our presentation suitable for a wider audience because we were able to offer stories and examples from the elementary EL specialist, high school content teacher, and administrator vantage points. Additionally, we divided the presentation so that we could each speak to the elements we had the most expertise or experience with, but we also took advantage of opportunities to add to each other's ideas.

It can be challenging to remember every little thing you plan to say in a formal presentation, but because we had practiced together, we were able to support one another in remembering key points in the event anything was accidentally left out. Because the SIOP model emphasizes interaction, conference sessions are expected to have interactive elements in which participants are conversing with one another and engaging in practice and application of the content being presented. We planned for interaction at several points during our presentation, and because there were three of us presenting, we were able to circulate and observe, listen, and chat with more participants than any of us could have managed individually. The first year we did the presentation, we fell short on time and ended up cutting some of our interactive portions. We were able to reflect as a team, and when we did the presentation a second time the following year, it was much improved based on our post-presentation discussions around the feedback we had received.

We found that the synergy that teachers get from collaborating on classroom instruction also existed when we'd planned collaboratively about professional development, and in a similar way, we were able to grow and enhance our understanding of our topics and practices beyond the parameters we would have had if we worked independently and then presented individually, one after the other. The positive effects of co-teaching also apply to collaborative professional development relationships, and I can say with confidence that I grew more as a teacher and as presenter after collaborating than I would have if I had only worked alone. Listening to other perspectives and seeing other styles really helped me refine my own.

Jess Bell
High School English Teacher

Co-Planning Instruction

There's a parable about a son who wanted to search for riches instead of being a farmer like his father. With a forlorn heart, the father bid safe travels to his ambitious son. The son traveled great distances and explored many lands, but after years of tireless unending travels, he returned home to his family empty-handed. The next morning, he went out to till the land with his father. As he was working, something twinkled under the soil. The son bent down to brush away the soil, and to his amazement, he found handfuls of gems. He frantically dug deeper, each shovelful revealing even more jewels. He had found, on the very land that was already in his family, the treasure that he had been searching for.

There are so many treasures to be found within the teachers in your school building. We can learn from our fellow educators in many ways, and the one we recommend is co-planning with them. Now more than ever, working in isolation is counterproductive. Co-planning is co-teaching, because co-teaching is the fruit of intentional co-planning. Without it, the expertise of the language specialist may not be utilized to the fullest extent possible. In order to best support multilingual learners, schools need to make the shift toward a shared sense of community and responsibility for these students, recognizing the need for collaboration between content teachers and language teachers in order to meet students' linguistic needs in all aspects of their schooling (Dove & Honigsfeld, 2017; TESOL, 2018; Toppel, 2018). Co-planning is a necessary component of the co-teaching cycle, but co-planning can also be a valuable collaboration even if instruction is not co-delivered.

Besides benefiting all students, co-planning also rewards the planners for engaging in this form of job-embedded learning. For example, language specialists can learn to better understand content-specific strategies from their content teacher co-planners. And the content teachers will add language-friendly scaffolds to their toolkits in the process. Both will benefit from the experience, developing affirming beliefs around multilingual learners and their families. Furthermore, co-planning forms professional learning communities that collaborate regularly to support multilingual learners – and that can be accessed simply by walking down the hall.

For those who do not have formal co-planning time scheduled with colleagues, we encourage you to ask your colleagues for their scope and sequence document or unit planners and collaborate asynchronously via email or by leaving comments and linking to resources. Additionally, you can do the same thing when asking about and planning for upcoming assessments that you won't have time to co-plan. Synchronous meetings are still truly where most of the gems lie, so it might be worth asking an administrator for additional, targeted planning time for you and your colleague either during the next professional development session or at another time during the school day.

Katie's Journey

The process of co-planning with other teachers has helped me become much more aware of grade-level expectations than I ever was when I planned alone. Through the expertise of grade-level teachers, I am able to fine-tune my ideas and lessons in order to ensure they are both linguistically and developmentally appropriate for particular age groups.

Carol's Journey

I have never found a content area teacher who wasn't willing to discuss multilingual learners over the copy machine. One example was Charlotte McHale, who shared students with me. One day we were discussing student progress in the workroom, and she handed me a copy of what she was doing with her English IV students to reinforce a lesson on themes. Using Michelle Obama's farewell speech with her grade-level students, she explained that the task would be for students to identify the theme of each paragraph. We quickly saw an opportunity for me to frontload overarching ideas for our shared students. For my own professional growth, I appreciated Charlotte's explanation of her lesson delivery, which helped me see a way to adapt the lesson for my newcomer classes.

Try It Out!

TEACHERS

- ☐ Partner with team members to deliver a workshop on a technique you have tried in your classrooms.
- ☐ Offer to join a team planning meeting.
- ☐ Embrace impromptu co-planning opportunities in the hallways, by the copier, or anywhere else.

COACHES

- ☐ Co-write an article for an existing blog.
- ☐ Partner with other coaches or teachers to present for your in-district and out-of-district events.
- ☐ Create and share tools that teachers can use to facilitate co-planning (template, agenda items, etc.).

ADMINISTRATORS

- ☐ Collaborate with another administrator, coach, or teacher on an article for your district's newsletter.
- ☐ Create and protect time for teachers to co-plan.
- ☐ Highlight faculty-led co-presentations.

Aspects to consider while reflecting on your learning.

DIRECTIONS
1. Choose a professional learning activity.
2. Evaluate that activity through the lens of each of these five aspects.
3. Mark on each line where the activity falls on the scale.

| Assigned learning activities | **CHOICE** | Self-selected learning activities |

| One-time learning experiences | **CONTINUITY** | Scheduled experiences throughout the year |

| Learning by yourself | **COMMUNITY** | Learning with colleagues |

| Learning about topics beyond your immediate need or context | **CONNECTEDNESS** | Learning about topics relevant to your context |

| Expensive | **COST** | Free |

REFLECT

- **Prioritize** your learning goals, and brainstorm ways to make your learning experiences more interactive.
- **Describe** how to make a recent interpretive learning experience more interactive.
- **Explain** the parallels between interactive learning experiences for students and interactive professional learning experiences for teachers.
- **Describe** how you could find others to support your interactive learning journey.
- **Create** a plan identifying your first three steps to becoming more interactive in your learning.

©Seidlitz Education. All rights reserved.

5

"Unless you try to do something beyond what you have already mastered, you will never grow."

| *Ronald E. Osborn, 1945*

EXTENDING PROFESSIONAL LEARNING

Our Journey

Not too long ago, the three of us were complete strangers. Now, we are forever connected as co-authors of this work, and more importantly, as friends. Our journeys have transformed us from individuals seeking professional learning opportunities to improve outcomes for multilingual learners to members of a fully collaborative, co-creating team. Consequently, we are individually more confident, more knowledgeable, and more prepared because our self-directed paths have converged. We are deeply grateful to have had so many opportunities to learn from, support, and lean on each other as we've pursued this work that is our heart and our passion.

The different paths we're sharing in this book are the paths we've taken personally that have transformed us individually and collectively, as educators, thinkers, and leaders. We are so happy that you are part of this journey too.

Because we connect, engage, and collaborate so extensively, we have been fortunate to learn from so many others who have shown us that the possibilities for professional learning are endless. As our world continues to change, shifts in education will be a natural outgrowth. Consequently, our learning will also be fluid and ongoing. The ways in which we approach professional learning will evolve constantly along with policy, technology, and humanity.

Not only are we committed to continuous learning, but we are also inspired to bring novelty and transformation to professional learning so that it stays relevant and meaningful in our ever-changing context. In our final chapter, we address the need to layer, lead, and innovate. These action words call us to rise to the challenge of carefully crafting opportunities to learn more deeply, to inspire others, and to take professional learning where it's never gone before.

Are you in?

Layer

The amount of information we remember increases substantially depending on how we engage in the learning process. This resource has taken you through a journey of professional learning opportunities as they align with interpretive, expressive, and interactive modes of learning. Each idea for professional learning offers a valid way to engage in reflection, growth, and improvement in professional practice; however, in order to convert that learning into heightened benefits and outcomes for our multilingual learners, it is necessary to extend the depth and breadth of our professional learning opportunities. As we move from interpretive learning opportunities (read, hear, watch) to interactive learning opportunities (discuss, experience, teach), we increase our potential to grow as educators and influence others so as to meaningfully impact their professional practice. This next section will show you how to expand upon the options presented in the previous chapters to truly supercharge your professional learning.

If you engage in any of this book's professional learning practices in isolation, you will likely find ways to enhance your teaching practice and improve outcomes for your MLLs. The key takeaway from options presented in this text is that your professional learning needs to align with your interests and needs so that you are invested in your own professional growth. Choice is imperative. However, we also encourage you to try out a variety of ways to access and interact with the topics you are choosing to learn more about. Through exploring various learning modalities, you can discover which learning pathways work best for you and which ones may not be a great fit.

Think of the ideas presented in this book like a trip itinerary. You plan out the destinations, the route to get there, and the activities you do in the mornings, afternoons, and evenings. All of these decisions add more enjoyment to your trip. Though staying at the beach all day is a fun way to spend a vacation, layering in many other activities makes it possible to build on the experience. With a little pre-planning, it's possible to schedule a surfing lesson in the morning, go snorkeling after lunch, attend a cooking class in the afternoon, walk along the beach at the sunset, and finally have dinner by the water. You can organize your professional learning itinerary similarly by thinking about the things you want to learn along the way, identifying experiences you want to participate in, and considering potential travel partners.

Choosing multiple learning opportunities and layering them together is a great way to supercharge your professional learning. Rather than focusing on a single learning avenue for your target growth areas, access information from multiple avenues, incorporating opportunities to interact and learn from others in the field. The term "pluriliteracies" refers to the many different ways students can engage in literacy above and beyond books (Helman et al., 2019). In addition to reading and writing, other multimodal manners of communication (e.g., visual, digital, technological, spatial, and audio) result in a wider variety of ways for students to show mastery of academic content. We encourage teachers to think of professional growth in a similar fashion.

Given an area of interest or specialty, you might layer your learning within a particular learning category (e.g., engage in several interpretive learning opportunities such as reading a book, listening to a podcast, and watching a video all on the same topic), or you might layer activities across different learning categories [e.g., listen to an audio book (which is interpretive), write a blog post (which is expressive), and join a Twitter chat to discuss the topic with colleagues (which is interactive)]. Layering activities together capitalizes on the varied retention rates associated with each so that you can move toward ownership and agency in your professional learning.

EXAMPLE 1: READ, CONNECT, WATCH

Anya, a third grade teacher, wanted to learn more about how to support her multilingual learners. So, she got a copy of *Growing Language and Literacy: Strategies for English Learners* (Honigsfeld, 2019) in order to learn more about what her students who were acquiring English were capable of at each level of proficiency. As she read, Anya made notes and highlighted the ideas she wanted to use for her students at the beginner level of language proficiency. Later, when she was scrolling through Twitter, she learned that a virtual book club was doing a slow chat about the book she had just read, so she joined in to discuss what she had learned with her Twitter PLN. She got some additional ideas about how to make content comprehensible for her beginning level students and was able to ask the author a question about one of the strategies she wanted to try. Anya incorporated two of the new ideas into her lesson plans and was excited to try them out. She decided to record her lesson so that she could watch her students to see how

> Choosing multiple learning opportunities and layering them together is a great way to supercharge your professional learning.

the new strategies worked for them. After school, Anya viewed the video and felt a bit disappointed that her students were still fairly quiet during her lesson. She returned to Twitter to share her experience, asking for suggestions about engaging her beginner students. A few colleagues encouraged her to keep trying and made suggestions for additional scaffolding. Someone suggested the need to provide students with sufficient time to think before asking them to talk. Another colleague in her PLN suggested that Anya could try providing students with visuals to use during partner talk in order to support them in showing classmates what they had learned. Anya wrote down the ideas, referred back to the book, and decided to record her lesson the following day. After school, Anya watched the video and was pleased to see that her beginning level students were more engaged in her lesson and that one of them even shared ideas during partner talk.

Analysis of Anya's Learning Experience

Though reading through the professional book (interpretive learning) helped Anya identify some new ideas, joining the Twitter chat to discuss them with her PLN (interactive learning) really helped her bring them to life. Recording herself trying the new strategies (interpretive) helped her track her progress, and reconnecting with her PLN for insight when she encountered obstacles (interactive) helped her fully affect her desired change. Although Anya's book was helpful in and of itself, the additions of a second interpretive pathway and an interactive pathway enhanced the learning from what she could have achieved with only one individual approach.

INTERPRETIVE	**Reading** a professional book
INTERACTIVE	**Connecting** with PLN and the author in a virtual book study
INTERPRETIVE	**Watching** video footage of a lesson based on suggestions from PLN
INTERACTIVE	**Reconnecting** with PLN to seek help
INTERPRETIVE	**Watching** additional lesson footage

EXAMPLE 2: WATCH, ENGAGE, CO-FACILITATE

Marcos, an instructional coach who supports K-12 language development teachers, planned to attend a virtual conference about teaching MLLs. Marcos was able to view different sessions from home, using the chat feature within the virtual delivery platform to engage in conversation with others who were viewing at the same time. He took particular interest in a session about vocabulary instruction and wanted to share the content with other instructional coaches in his district. Marcos invited five content-area instructional coaches to a watch party so the group could view the presentation together and discuss the strategies for vocabulary instruction that were included. The group came up with a list of three key action items for vocabulary instruction that they wanted to share with content teachers during summer professional learning sessions. Marcos worked with each content-area coach to create a short presentation reflecting the vocabulary action items with specific examples from their content specialities. Then Marcos co-facilitated each presentation in order to bring the language acquisition lens to the discussion and to answer questions about vocabulary instruction as it pertains to multilingual learners in respective content areas.

Analysis of Marcos' Learning Experience

Marcos started his professional learning with the interpretive path but quickly made it interactive by engaging with other viewers in real time during the virtual presentations and sharing the viewing experience with his colleagues to broaden his learning. By initiating collaboration across different departments, Marcos encouraged colleagues to understand vocabulary instruction as it applies to students acquiring a new language so that they can experience the benefits of the key instructional practices across content areas. Through cross-content collaboration, instructional coaches were able to learn from one another. Marcos was also able to provide support and expertise during presentations to content-area teachers in order to broaden their learning by emphasizing how effective approaches to language instruction apply within the context of their instruction.

INTERPRETIVE	**Watching** a virtual conference
INTERACTIVE	**Engaging** virtually with participants during conference sessions
INTERACTIVE	**Watching** and discussing with colleagues
INTERACTIVE	**Co-facilitating** subsequent PD sessions for teachers

EXAMPLE 3: LISTEN, CREATE, COLLABORATE, PRESENT

Taylor, a middle school science teacher, wanted to learn more about supporting their multilingual learners in writing about science topics. They found an episode of Larry Ferlazzo's Classroom Q&A podcast (Ferlazzo, 2018) that highlighted some useful ideas about teaching writing within the discipline of science. They listened to the short episode on the way to work and made note of some ideas about how they could support their MLLs in content-specific writing tasks. During their prep time, Taylor sketchnoted the main points from the Classroom Q&A episode and brought their notes to some of their language specialist colleagues to ask for support. They asked their two colleagues for additional ideas about how to incorporate more writing into their science lessons and how to provide scaffolds for students at beginning and intermediate levels of English proficiency. Working together, the three educators came up with a short menu of options for writing tasks to incorporate during science and a second menu of scaffolds that would benefit learners at different language proficiency levels. Taylor then shared the lists with other science teachers at a department meeting so they too could benefit from the expertise of the language specialists and writing teachers.

Analysis of Taylor's Learning Experience

Taylor enjoys listening to educational podcasts, so it made sense for them to search for a podcast episode on supporting their diverse students. They found a quick way to fit this interpretive learning into their busy schedule by listening during their work commute. They then chose an expressive pathway by creating graphics to summarize and support recall of what they learned. Taylor shifted from expressive to interactive learning by initiating collaboration with their colleagues who had expertise in writing and by collaborating with them to produce a lesson based on the writing ideas and the science content. Taylor came away from the collaboration with some great new tools and decided to add another layer to their professional learning by presenting the valuable tools to other science teachers. In order to prepare the presentation, they had to further solidify their own learning so they could clearly communicate what the tools are, why they were created, and how they can be used.

INTERPRETIVE		**Listening** to a podcast
EXPRESSIVE		**Creating** sketchnotes to capture the main points from the Classroom Q&A episode
INTERACTIVE		**Collaborating** with colleagues to create curriculum documents
EXPRESSIVE		**Presenting** ideas to other colleagues in the science department

EXAMPLE 4: WATCH, CHOOSE BETWEEN MULTIPLE PATHS, INTERACT

Dr. Yang, an elementary school principal, wanted to support her staff in learning more about being culturally responsive educators. She brought in an educational consultant, Dr. Michelle Yzquierdo, author of *Pathways to Greatness for ELL Newcomers*, to present about culturally responsive teaching during a teacher in-service professional learning day.

Following the presentation, Dr. Yang created a choice board for teachers on her staff in order to provide subsequent professional learning opportunities. She asked each teacher to select three different choices to try out and then provided time at staff meetings for teachers to connect and discuss what they had done and what they had learned.

INTERPRETIVE	EXPRESSIVE	INTERACTIVE
Read an article	Create a graphic to capture your learning	Talk with a colleague about culturally responsive teaching strategies they've tried
Watch a webinar on culturally responsive teaching	Write a journal reflection about takeaways from the training	Co-plan a lesson with a colleague and reflect together afterward
Listen to students of color give their perspectives on school	Present reflections from a lesson at a staff meeting	Collaborate with students to plan for different options for a content-related culminating project

Analysis of Dr. Yang's Staff Development Plan

Dr. Yang wanted to make sure that her staff had a chance to learn from an expert in the field, so the first step of her plan was to provide an interpretive learning opportunity. The additional opportunities she provided gave teachers a chance to deepen their learning from the initial training, and by creating time for teachers to continue to engage with one another, she empowered them to bring their learning into the classroom and help one another refine their new strategies.

INTERPRETIVE		**Watching** an educational consultant model strategies
EXPRESSIVE		**Creating** a choice board for her teachers to use, including a sample of one item from each column of the choice board
INTERACTIVE		**Engaging** in choice board activities
INTERACTIVE		**Discussing** choice board tasks with colleagues

Example 5: Read, Watch, Create, Connect & Engage

Kelly, a fifth grade teacher at Dr. Yang's school, learned that she and her colleagues would attend a presentation about culturally responsive teaching. She researched the presenter and read an article to build some background knowledge before attending the workshop. During the presentation, Kelly took notes about the salient points and created sketchnotes to help remember what she learned. As she began to implement some of the new ideas, she journaled about her lessons and reflected on how culturally responsive instructional methods positively affected her students. Kelly became very curious about how her multilingual learners were receiving the changes in her instruction, so she opted to try out two more ideas from Dr. Yang's choice board. First she took part in a Twitter chat to gain more insights about culturally responsive teaching practices from other teachers in her PLN. Then she had one-on-one conversations with several of her students to learn more about their experiences and perspectives with regards to her instruction. She really enjoyed learning from her students and decided to invite them to collaborate with her to think of different ideas for how they could show their learning for their final project for the semester.

Analysis of Kelly's Learning Experience

While Dr. Yang offered her staff multiple learning opportunities, Kelly is an educator who often drives her own professional growth. By previewing the training content prior to the in-service day (interpretive), she laid a foundation to deepen her learning, and she built on that further by creating visual notes throughout the training (expressive). The interpretive and interactive opportunities she selected from the choice board helped her build on her newly acquired strategies by gathering feedback and additional perspectives. Kelly's learning experience could have remained exclusively interpretive, however due to Dr. Yang's leadership and her personal initiative, she layered together multiple paths to truly enhance her professional growth.

INTERPRETIVE	**Reading** an article on a professional learning topic
INTERPRETIVE	**Watching** an educational consultant model strategies
EXPRESSIVE	**Creating** notes with graphics
EXPRESSIVE	**Writing** journal entries about culturally responsive lessons
INTERACTIVE	**Engaging** in a Twitter Chat about culturally responsive teaching practices with PLN to learn more **Collaborating** with students to think of different ideas to show all they've learned in a final project

Each of the previous scenarios is an example of what it can look like to layer professional learning opportunities in order to broaden learning by engaging through different modalities. Each layer offers a unique opportunity to sustain learning and contributes to increased understanding and competency by drawing from different sources of information that can offer support and expertise for teaching MLLs. Layered learning can be done independently, but as you incorporate different elements into your learning, it is important to consider ways to connect with others. Collaborative efforts have the potential for wider and more nuanced learning, which eventually results in greater benefits for the students we serve.

Lead

ANYONE CAN LEAD

There are many different conceptualizations and styles of leadership, but being a leader is not necessarily the same as being the boss. While we certainly rely on the quality leadership of administrators and others in educational leadership roles, we also know that anyone can be a leader. Leadership is not confined to certain roles, nor is it limited to particular spaces. In the context of professional learning, leaders are often those who are brave, inspiring, passionate, willing to take action, and not afraid to fail.

As Brené Brown (2018) says, "A brave leader is not someone who is armed with all the answers" (p.195). Leaders are those who have the tenacity to keep trying even when success is not immediate. Naturally, we'd rather share about experiences that went amazingly well, but being transparent and honest about the less than stellar moments normalizes the idea that every educator has room to grow. Leadership is a willingness to take the risk. Being a leader is just as much associated with the intent as it is with the outcome.

VULNERABILITY BUILDS TRUST

Covey's idea of interdependence (see p. 68 in Interactive) goes hand in hand with the vulnerability and humility of recognizing that as individuals, we do not have all the answers, but as communities, we can leverage multiple perspectives and talents in order to make a more substantial impact on multilingual learners. Brown (2018) affirms the value of interdependence, highlighting the need for a culture of trust, openness, collaboration, and a shift toward a mentality of continuous learning.

> **Leadership is not confined to certain roles, nor is it limited to particular spaces.**

Often, we want to be the superheroes who can do it all, but recognizing that we need each other is essential for doing the kind of collaborative work that will truly turn the dial for students. We frequently affirm that we are "better together" because we know that it takes a collective effort to foster positive change. In our work, we must find our inner circles and enter into a cycle of continuous learning and collective growth with other brave educators. We do this work with the intention of expanding the circle in order to guide and support students and other educators on a wider level. In return, we experience the benefit of guidance and support from our ever-growing circles, whose members offer multiple perspectives and vantage points that contribute to more nuanced learning and leadership.

As you continue in the exciting work of engaging and leading others in their own journeys of professional learning, it can be helpful to remember that there isn't any one specific path to success; each person will engage in ways that feel intriguing, exciting, and motivating for them. Our job as leaders in this work is to lead with openness, to listen, to continue learning, and to think outside the box in order to sustain a continuous cycle of learning.

FIND POCKETS OF SUCCESS

Sometimes seeing oneself as a leader is a challenge. We recognize and admire leadership in others around us, but we neglect to see it within ourselves and are quick to doubt our personal contributions as integral to initiating change. Bravery and vulnerability are key to surpassing our discomfort and doubt. Brown's four big P's (trying to prove ourselves, be perfect, perform, and please) can be barriers, but we need to step into that zone of discomfort and embrace uncertainty, because that is where both personal and collective growth occur (2018). In her VirtuEL17 keynote presentation, (see the QR code below), Nancy Motley, author of *Talk, Read, Talk, Write*, encourages us to find "pockets of success" (2017). She describes the positive effects small victories can have on motivation and reminds us to recognize that small successes over time build the momentum for larger impact.

Consider this scenario to examine how our perceptions of ourselves as leaders may not accurately reflect the reality of our impact.

Perception: At a weekly staff meeting, you present a strategy you have been using to support multilingual learners in reading complex texts. While showing a few slides to model how it works, you notice some colleagues are disengaged and others are checking email. You leave the meeting feeling discouraged, thinking nobody cared.

Reality: Some teachers did care. Some may have felt overwhelmed at the idea of learning something new. Some may not use your strategy. Some may not have even been listening. But a few teachers liked what they heard and wanted to try it. One teacher made a note of the idea in her lesson plan book. Another reached out to ask you a follow-up question. A third asked for more information.

If your presentation resulted in a few teachers trying something new, or even just being open to trying something new, your efforts were not in vain! Those teachers who try out your strategy might mention it to a teammate or talk about it in the staff room, and their success and interest will likely spread to others. Even if, initially, only a few colleagues become your allies in professional learning, that still can be a great foundation on which to build. If each teacher partners with additional teachers and continues to guide, lead, and support, the effect of your leadership will be magnified.

Some recent examples of inspiring leadership:
Maria Montroni-Currais created two weeks of tech-free, at-home lesson plans for multilingual learners during the COVID-19 pandemic. Her plans quickly gained popularity and were subsequently translated into many languages with the help of multilingual teachers from across the country.

ESL at Home

"About the project: ESL at Home began as a simple, two-week activity calendar for the ELLs in my district of Somerdale, New Jersey. With the help of teachers in Fort Mill, South Carolina, I added two more weeks. I shared it on Facebook and Twitter and was offered assistance in translating it into Spanish. That led me to ask on social media for more translations, and in less than three weeks, we had 20 translations. Since I started this project, educators from all over the country have collaborated to translate or share. I'm so thrilled to have been part of a project that has positively impacted students all over the globe."

Maria Montroni-Currais
School Administrator

for Educators of Multilingual Learners 105

Laura Baker brought Tan's idea of *Bathroom Briefs* to her school in order to support teachers and provide information "on the go." She met the needs of the teachers at her school by asking them what information they were interested in, then created custom graphics to support their areas of need.

"Twitter has been great for professional learning. One moment of inspiration was stumbling upon Tan Huynh's *Bathroom Briefs*. As an ESL team, we rarely get the opportunity to share best practices with the staff. I thought his *Bathroom Briefs* would be a great way to impart knowledge in working with ELs, who make up about a quarter of our student population. The first year, I used Tan's *Bathroom Briefs*, focusing on different language levels and types of scaffolds. They were well received, especially by the administrators. Rather than repeat the *Bathroom Briefs* for the next year, I decided to create my own, with encouragement from Tan.

My initial learning curve was using the technology to create the actual document. From there, I was able to create many different tools for ELs using Google Drawings. It's easy once you learn how! My state was introducing language standards for the classroom. I introduced the document, the anchor standards, and how to look closely at each strand, as well as the different expectations based on the language level. These were differentiated by "bathroom wing." The fifth grade teachers only saw the fourth and fifth grade band of standards, etc. This was an eight-week series, and it opened the door for conversation with classroom teachers. Following this, I created briefs with key points from several professional texts I've read and enjoyed. As I gained the knowledge, I shared it with the staff.

This year, now that I can easily create my own documents, I asked the staff what they wanted to learn. I left some sticky notes and pens with the first *Bathroom Brief* of the year, along with a request for feedback. One request was for math vocabulary teaching strategies. In order to teach, I had to learn/review myself. I scoured my resources and searched the internet for best practices and visual examples. I created a plan to deliver the information in an organized way, focusing on topics such as assessment, polysemous words, and word problems. Again, I have received positive feedback from administrators as well as staff. We are all learning together."

Laura Baker
ESL Teacher

Bathroom Briefs
ESL Strategies on-the-go, as you go

Use a rating chart so Ss can self-assess and Ts can plan vocabulary instruction.

Word	Know It, Can Explain It	Have Heard It or Seen It	Do Not Know This
Square	X		
Rectangle	X		
Rhombus			X
Quadrilateral		X	
Trapezoid			X

You can include ratings such as:
1. I don't recognize this word.
2. I recognize the word, but I don't know what it means.
3. I have a basic understanding of the word.
4. I understand the word and can teach it to others.

GOALS

A teacher on Twitter @ConnieMtz uses Flipgrid to create "Live Word Walls". The grids are set up by topic. When students are struggling with a topic, they are able to watch a classmate explain it to them at any time by scanning the QR code.

Imagine the impact on McKinley students!!!

Dorina Ebuwa, Educational Consultant for B.E.L.I.E.V.E.! LLC created #BELIEVE_cafe to support teachers through a journey of self-care and emotional intelligence during distance learning.

Dorina Ebuwa (Miss Dorito)
@Dorina_BELIEVE

Excited 4 tomorrow morning! Join me as we begin our journey of self care, happiness, vulnerability, real talk & the power of transformative emotional intelligence. Now more than ever, we need to understand the WHY of our feelings and the HOW if dealing with them. See u tomorrow!

ENCOURAGE

One more action verb should be considered as an integral part of leadership: encourage. It is important to emphasize the power of praise, validation, and recognition. When we cultivate relationships with colleagues, mentors, experts, and administrators, we must bear in mind that everyone appreciates feeling valued and it is imperative that we root for each other. As educators, we work tirelessly for our students. We certainly did not choose this profession for fame or fortune, but we do want our efforts to be seen and appreciated. We owe it to each other to take on the responsibility of lifting one another up in order to breathe positivity and empowerment into our work.

It is important for us to be attentive and observant and to seek out ways to recognize others, because "when people feel and know they are valued and make a significant impact on an organization, they routinely strive to not only perform at peak levels, but also improve their skills so they can make a greater difference in the future" (Kuczmarski & Kuczmarski, 2018, p.4). Casas (2020) says, "When we all intentionally lift each other up, we build a sense of community among the staff where we all can be celebrated and honored for striving to do what we expect kids to do everyday: our very best" (p. 73).

Innovate

Previous chapters have provided many different pathways for professional learning, but this book does not contain all the answers. It is our hope that these ideas will help you and those in your circle get started. It is also our hope that you will come up with ideas of your own that make sense in your particular context. To be innovative is, in a sense, to be creative. We don't want to limit your scope or suggest there is a particular path for innovation. This is where you take the wheel and navigate new territory. It's time to get creative and innovate!

Zwiers (2019) breaks down the concept of creativity when discussing how to amplify the authenticity of communication in student learning. He identifies four dimensions to consider when teachers aim to infuse more authentic communication into their lesson: **discovering, problem solving, expressing,** and **interpreting**. There is a parallel between what he is asking of teachers for the sake of improved student learning experiences and what we are recommending in this book to improve professional learning experiences for educators. Zwiers encourages educators to embrace creativity in order to understand "what our students need to learn, what they have learned, what they want to learn, how they learn, and who they are" (p.174). These exact ideas apply to the need to amplify, extend, and personalize the ways educators engage with professional learning. In order to extend your own journey of creative thinking, it might be helpful to explore Zwiers' dimensions, applying them to the innovation of new ideas for professional learning in your personal context.

Discover: Educator Self-Reflection

- What are my areas of interest?
- What strengths do I possess?
- What are the areas in which I need to grow?
- Which pathway for learning do I connect with the most?
- What new ways of learning do I want to try?
- With whom do I want to learn?

Problem Solve: Investigate Current Barriers

- When/why am I lacking motivation?
- In what ways could communication or collaboration be improved?
- In what ways could professional development activities/procedures be modified to better meet my needs/the needs of my colleagues?
- What perspectives do I have?
- Which other voices need to be heard/included?

Express: Communicate and Compare

- Discuss self-reflections with others.
- Ask for feedback.
- Set intentions.
- Write goals.
- Express concerns.
- Ask what colleagues want and need.

Interpret: Process and Innovate

- What actions can I layer together to make professional learning more relevant for me and my colleagues?
- How can I connect different paths to maximize learning?
- What will work for me and/or my particular setting?
- What new ideas do I have?

Zwiers concludes with a powerful statement about empowering students:

For too long we have treated students as consumers of ideas. Instead our goal should be to see them as architects, engineers, designers, builders, and owners of ideas. It's time to enhance how and what students learn in order to realize this goal. Our students' abilities to learn, create, think, and communicate deserve to be more respected and valued in every classroom. They need to be – and yearn to be – in classrooms where they can build up ideas with others as they also build lasting relationships, language abilities, and social skills (p.179).

Just as we so wholeheartedly want this vision for our students, we find ourselves craving the same validation, voice, and flexibility in our own learning so that we can make it a reality for them in return.

When it comes to your own journey with professional learning, don't be afraid to break new ground. Many of the learning opportunities we've discussed thus far are the result of innovators coming up with new ideas for the sake of their own learning or to support the learning of others. In doing what works for you, you will be able to magnify your impact by finding ways to make professional learning fun and engaging for yourself and others.

We are all in this together.

Aspects to consider while reflecting on your learning.

DIRECTIONS
1. Choose a professional learning activity.
2. Evaluate that activity through the lens of each of these five aspects.
3. Mark on each line where the activity falls on the scale.

| Assigned learning activities | CHOICE | Self-selected learning activities |

| One-time learning experiences | CONTINUITY | Scheduled experiences throughout the year |

| Learning by yourself | COMMUNITY | Learning with colleagues |

| Learning about topics beyond your immediate need or context | CONNECTEDNESS | Learning about topics relevant to your context |

| Expensive | COST | Free |

REFLECT

- **Evaluate** the benefits of layering different professional learning paths together.
- **Describe** learning activities that could be layered together for an optimal learning experience.
- **Analyze** which paths have been missing from your professional learning and why.
- **Describe** your strengths or skills that can be leveraged to lead the professional learning of others.
- **Create** an innovative idea for professional learning.

The Authors

Katie Toppel, EdD is a K-5 Language Development Specialist primarily supporting students in kindergarten and first grade through co-planning, co-teaching, and small group instruction. Her background includes experience as an adjunct professor at Portland State University and as a classroom teacher in preschool, kindergarten, and first grade. Dr. Toppel co-created #MLLChat_BkClub with Tan Huynh and leads book studies for teachers continuing their professional learning on topics related to culturally and linguistically diverse students.

Tan Huynh is an educator specializing in providing sheltered instruction for multilingual learners. He received his M.A.Ed from the American College of Education specializing in Language Acquisition Instruction. Tan spent most of his career collaborating with teachers from elementary to high school levels to make content accessible before becoming a secondary social studies teacher himself. He has contributed articles to Middle Web, Larry Ferlazzo's Edweek blog, and WIDA International, as well as numerous other publications. Tan maintains a blog, podcast, and online courses for teachers of MLLs.

Carol Salva is a consultant at Seidlitz Education and the co-author of *Boosting Achievement: Reaching Students with Interrupted or Minimal Education*. She specializes in teaching grade level content to new arrival students. Carol has a background in ESL, literacy, dual language, and special education. She is a former elementary and middle school educator. She most recently taught Newcomer English Language Development in high school where she has had proven success with remote and asynchronous activities.

BIBLIOGRAPHY

Anderson, L. W., & Bloom, B. S. (2001). *A taxonomy for learning, teaching, and assessing: A revision of Bloom's taxonomy of educational objectives.* Longman.

Ayas, K. & Zeniuk, N. (2001). Project-based learning: Building communities of reflective practitioners. *Management Learning, 32,* 61-76.

Bada, S. O., & Olusegun, S. (2015). Constructivism learning theory: A paradigm for teaching and learning. *Journal of Research & Method in Education,* 5(6), 66-70. DOI: 10.9790/7388-05616670

Bailey, K. M. (1990). The use of diary studies in teacher education programs. In Richards, J. C., Richards, J. C., & Nunan, D. (Eds.). *Second language teaching education* (pp. 215-240). Cambridge University Press.

Bandura, A. (1977). Self-efficacy: Toward a unifying theory of behavioral change. *Psychological review,* 84(2), 191. https://www.uky.edu/~eushe2/Bandura/Bandura1977PR.pdf

Bill & Melinda Gates Foundation. (2014). Teachers know best: *Teachers' views on professional development* (ED576976). ERIC. https://files.eric.ed.gov/fulltext/ED576976.pdf

Bishop, R. S. (1990). Mirrors, windows, and sliding glass doors. *Perspectives: Choosing and using books for the classroom,* 6(3), ix-xi.

Bishop, R.S. (2015, Jan 30). *Mirrors, windows and sliding glass doors* [Video]. Reading Rockets. https://www.readingrockets.org/teaching/experts/rudine-sims-bishop

Boland Jr, R. J., & Tenkasi, R. V. (1995). Perspective making and perspective taking in communities of knowing. *Organization science,* 6(4), 350-372.

Boushey, G., & Moser, J. (2014). *The daily 5: Fostering literacy independence in the elementary grades.* Stenhouse Publishers.

Brown, B. (2018). *Dare to lead: Brave work. Tough conversations. Whole hearts.* Random House.

Burton, J., Quirke, P., Reichmann, C. L., & Peyton, J. K. (Eds.). (2009). *Reflective writing. A way to lifelong teacher learning.* TESL-EJ Publications.

Cain, S. (2012, March 2). *The power of introverts* [Video]. TED. https://www.ted.com/talks/susan_cain_the_power_of_introverts?language=en

Cakir, H. (2013). Use of blogs in pre-service teacher education to improve student engagement. *Computers & Education,* 68(1), 244-252. doi.org/10.1016/j.compedu.2013.05.013

Calderón, M.E., Dove, M.G., Fenner, D.S., Gottlieb, M., Honigsfeld, A., Singer, T.W., Slakk, S., Soto, I., Zacarian, D. (2019). *Breaking down the wall: Essential shifts for English learner success.* Corwin.

Center for Advanced Research on Language Acquisition (CARLA). (2019, April 9). The Center for Advanced Research on Language Acquisition: Assessment of Second Language. https://carla.umn.edu/assessment/vac/CreateUnit/step4_interpretive.html

Casas, J. (2020). *Live your excellence: Bring your best self to school everyday*. Dave Burgess Consulting, Inc.

Choi, Y. (2013). *The name jar*. Zaner-Bloser.

Cisneros, S., (2010). *The house on mango street* (Bloom, H. Ed.). Bloom's Literary Criticism.

Clark, R. C., & Mayer, R. E. (2016). *E-learning and the science of instruction: Proven guidelines for consumers and designers of multimedia learning*. John Wiley & Sons.

Cohan, A., Honigsfeld, A., & Dove, M. G. (2019). *Team up, speak up, fire up!: Educators, students, and the community working together to support English learners*. Association for Supervision & Curriculum Development.

Collins, K. (2004). *Growing readers: Units of study in the primary classroom*. Stenhouse Publishers.

Conkling, W. (2013). *Sylvia & Aki*. Yearling.

Covey, S. (1989). *The 7 habits of highly effective people*. Simon and Schuster.

Covey, S. R. (2020). *The 7 habits of highly effective people: Revised and updated: Powerful lessons in personal change*. Simon & Schuster.

Davison, C. (2006). Collaboration between ESL and content teachers: How do we know when we are doing it right?. *International Journal of Bilingual Education and Bilingualism, 9*(4), 454-475.

Day, C. (1999). Researching teaching through reflective practice. In Loughran, J. (Ed.), Researching teaching: *Methodologies and practices for understanding pedagogy* (pp. 215-232). Falmer Press.

Dean, C. B., & Hubbell, E. R. (2012). *Classroom instruction that works: Research-based strategies for increasing student achievement*. Ascd.

de Moor, A., & Efimova, L. (2004). An argumentation analysis of weblog conversations. In *Proceedings of the 9th international working conference on the language-action perspective on communication modelling (LAP 2004)* (pp. 197-212). International Working Conference on the LAP on Communication.

Deng, L., & Yuen, A. H. (2013). Blogs in pre-service teacher education: Exploring the participation issue. *Technology, Pedagogy and Education, 22*(3), 339-356. doi.org/10.1080/1475939X.2013.802990

Deslauriers, L., Schelew, E., & Wieman, C. (2011). Improved learning in a large-enrollment physics class. *Science, 332*(6031), 862-864.

Dewey, J. (1933). *How we think*. D. C. Heath and Co.

Dove, M. G., & Honigsfeld, A. (2017). *Co-teaching for English learners: A guide to collaborative planning, instruction, assessment, and reflection* (1st ed.). Corwin.

Downes, S. (2004). *Educational blogging. Educause*, 39(5), 14-26.

Echevarria, J., Vogt, M., & Short, D. (2017). *Making content comprehensible for English learners: The SIOP model* (5th ed.). Pearson Education, Inc.

Efimova, L., & Fiedler, S. (2004, March). Learning webs: Learning in weblog networks. In *Proceedings of the IADIS International Conference Web Based Communities* (pp. 490-494).

Elliott, S. N., Kratochwill, T. R., Littlefield Cook, J., & Travers, J. (2000). *Educational psychology: Effective teaching, effective learning* (3rd ed.). McGraw-Hill.

Farrell, T. S. C. (2008). Reflective practice in the professional development of teachers of adult English language learners. CAELA Network Brief. *Center for Adult English Language Acquisition (CAELA)*. www.cal.org/caelanetwork/resources/reflectivepractice.html

Farrell, T. S. C. (2015a). It's not who you are! It's how you teach! Critical competencies associated with effective teaching. *RELC Journal*, 46(1), 79-88. https://doi.org/10.1177/0033688214568096

Farrell, T. S. C. (2015b). *Promoting teacher reflection in second language education: A framework for TESOL professionals*. Routledge.

Ferlazzo, L. (Host). (2018, Mar 31). Integrating writing skills into your science class. [Audio podcast episode]. In *Classroom Q&A with Larry Ferlazzo*. BAM! Radio. https://www.bamradionetwork.com/track/integrating-writing-skills-development-into-your-science-class/

Fernandes, M., Wammes, J., & Meade, M. (2018). The Surprisingly Powerful Influence of Drawing on Memory. *Current Directions in Psychological Science*, 27(5), 302-308.

Finlay, L. (2008). Reflecting on 'reflective practice'. Practice-based Professional Learning Paper 52, 1-27. T*he Open University*.

Fiorella, L., & Mayer, R. E. (2014). Role of expectations and explanations in learning by teaching. *Contemporary Educational Psychology*, 39(2), 75-85.

Francis, E. (2019, July. 16). *Building bridges* [Conference session]. SIOP National Conference, Portland, OR.

Freire, P. (2007). *Pedagogy of the oppressed*. The Continuum International Publishing Group Inc.

Fujii, T. (2016). Designing and adapting tasks in lesson planning: a critical process of lesson study. *ZDM*, 4(48), 411-423.

Fulwiler, T. & Young, A. (1982). Introduction. In Fulwiler, T., & Young, A. (Eds.), Language connections: *Writing and reading across the curriculum* (pp. ix-xiii). National Council of Teachers of English.

Garrison, D. R. (1997). Self-directed learning: Toward a comprehensive model. *Adult Education Quarterly*, 48(1), 18-33.

Gay, G. (2010). *Culturally responsive teaching: Theory, research, and practice* (2nd ed.). Teachers College Press.

Gee, J. P. (2001). Identity as an analytic lens for research in education. *Review of Research in Education*, 25, 99-125.

Gewertz, C. (2019, December 10). *How much should teachers talk in the classroom? Much less, some say.* Education Week. https://www.edweek.org/leadership/how-much-should-teachers-talk-in-the-classroom-much-less-some-say/2019/12

González, N., Moll, L. C., & Amanti, C. (Eds.). (2006). *Funds of knowledge: Theorizing practices in households, communities, and classrooms.* Routledge.

Gratz, A. (2020). *Refugee.* Thorndike Press.

Halla Jmourko [@HallaJmourko]. (2018, February 12). *I'd to share a tool I developed emphasizing the need of situating #scaffolding #LD Supports in #LearningEnvironment inclusive of diversity. #ELLs who engage when supported in comprehension of & communication during lessons. #LD Supports are extended to include Verbal & Textual.* [Image attached] [Tweet]. Twitter. https://twitter.com/HallaJmourko/status/962743850686124032

Hammond, Z., & Jackson, Y. (2015). *Culturally responsive teaching and the brain: Promoting authentic engagement and rigor among culturally and linguistically diverse students.* Corwin.

Harvey, S., & Ward, A. (2017). *From striving to thriving: How to grow confident, capable readers.* Scholastic Teaching Resources.

Hattie, J. (2009) *Visible learning: A synthesis of over 800 meta-analyses relating to achievement.* Routledge.

Helman, L., Ittner, A. C., & McMaster, K. L. (2019). *Assessing language and literacy with bilingual students: Practices to support English learners.* Guilford Publications.

Hiebert, E. H., & Reutzel, D. R. (2010). Revisiting silent reading in 2020 and beyond. In *Revisiting silent reading: New directions for teachers and researchers.* International Reading Association, 290-299.

Hines, M. (2008). Using blogging as a tool to further teacher professional development. In *Proceedings of TCC 2008* (pp. 152-162). TCCHawaii. http://hdl.handle.net/10125/69271

Honigsfeld, A. (2019). *Growing language and literacy.* Heinemann.

Honigsfeld, A., & Dove, M. G. (2010). *Collaboration and co-teaching: Strategies for English learners.* Corwin.

Honigsfeld, A., & Dove, M. G. (2019). *Collaborating for English learners: A foundational guide to integrated practices* (2nd ed.). Corwin.

International Baccalaureate Organization. (2015). *Diploma History Guide* (pp. 1-98). International Baccalaureate Organization.

International Society for Technology in Education. (2018, August 24). *ISTE Standards for Educators.* https://www.iste.org/standards/for-educators

Jennifer: Advice on blogging [E-mail to the author]. (2019, August 8).

Jiménez, F. (2002). *The circuit stories from the life of a migrant child.* Univ. of New Mexico Press.

Johnson, D.W., & Johnson, R.T. (2009). An educational psychology success story: Social interdependence theory and cooperative learning. *Educational Researcher, 38*(5), 365-379. https://doi.org/10.3102/0013189X09339057

Justin: Blogging contribution [E-mail to the author]. (2019, August 14).

Kagan, S. (2010). Excellence & equity. *Kagan Online Magazine*, Summer 2010. www.kaganonline.com/free_articles/dr_spencer_kagan/266/Excellence-amp-Equity

Kolb, D. A., & Fry, R. E. (1974). *Toward an applied theory of experiential learning*. MIT Alfred P. Sloan School of Management.

Krathwohl, D. R. (2002). A revision of Bloom's taxonomy: An overview. *Theory into practice*, 41(4), 212-218.

Kuczmarski, S.S., & Kuczmarski, T.D. (2018). *Lifting people up: The power of recognition*. Book Ends Publishing.

Lankow, J., Ritchie, J., & Crooks, R. (2012). Infographics: *The power of visual storytelling*. John Wiley & Sons.

Larry's contribution (blogging) [E-mail to the author]. (2019, August 13).

Larry's contribution (guest blogging) [E-mail to the author]. (2019, September 20).

Lee, H. J. (2005). Understanding and assessing preservice teachers' reflective thinking. *Teaching and teacher education*, 21(6), 699-715. https://doi.org/10.1016/j.tate.2005.05.007

Luehmann, A. L. (2008). Using blogging in support of teacher professional identity development: A case study. *The Journal of the Learning Sciences*, 17(3), 287-337. https://doi.org/10.1080/10508400802192706

Martin, T. (n.d., August 23). #BookSnaps - Snapping for Learning. *Be Real*. https://www.tarammartin.com/booksnaps-snapping-for-learning/

Mayer, R. E. (2014). Multimedia instruction. In Spector, J. M., Merrill, M. D., Elen, J., & Bishop, M. J. (Eds.). *Handbook of research on educational communications and technology* (pp. 413-424). Springer.

McCandless, D. (2010, July). *The beauty of data visualizations* [Video]. TED Conferences. https://www.ted.com/talks/david_mccandless_the_beauty_of_data_visualization?language=en#t-904169

Mercer, N. (1995). *The guided construction of knowledge: Talk amongst teachers and learners*. Multilingual Matters.

Merriam-Webster. (n.d.). Interactive. In *Merriam-Webster.com dictionary*. Retrieved December 28, 2019, from https://www.merriam-webster.com/dictionary/interactive.

Mirel, J., & Goldin, S. (2012, April 17). Alone in the classroom: Why teachers are too isolated. *The Atlantic*. https://www.theatlantic.com/national/archive/2012/04/alone-in-the-classroom-why-teachers-are-too-isolated/255976/

Harun, H., Shaari, N., & Othman, A. (2018). Infographic as a tool to Facilitate Teaching and Learning. In Mohamad, B., Imam Omoloso, A., Ridwan Adetunji, R., Memon, S., & Harun, H. (Eds.). *Proceedings of the SMMTC Postgraduate Symposium 2018*, (pp 99-103). UUM Press. https://www.researchgate.net/publication/326741487_SMMTC_Postgraduate_Proceedings_2018

Moll, L. C., Amanti, C., Neff, D., & Gonzalez, N. (1992). Funds of knowledge for teaching: Using a qualitative approach to connect homes and classrooms. *Theory Into Practice*, 31(2), 132-141. http://www.jstor.org/stable/1476399

Montroni-Currais, M. (2020). ESL at home: *12 weeks, tech free*. ESL at Home. https://eslathome.edublogs.org/

Motley, N. (2017, June 17). *Be brave! A return to the basics* [Video]. Youtube. https://www.youtube.com/watch?v=44dC4DYPtM4

National Education Association, Learning Forward, & Corwin. (2017). *The state of teacher professional learning: Results from a nationwide survey*. Corwin. https://us.corwin.com/sites/default/files/professional_learning_teacher_survey_2017.pdf

Nolan, J., & Hoover, L. (2008). *Teacher supervision and evaluation: Theory into practice* (2nd ed.). John Wiley & Sons.

November, A. C. (2012). *Who owns the learning? Preparing students for success in the digital age*. Solution Tree Press.

Paivio, A. (1971). *Imagery and verbal processes*. Holt, Rinehart & Winston.

Paivio, A., & Csapo, K. (1973). Picture superiority in free recall: Imagery or dual coding?. *Cognitive Psychology*. 5(2), 176-206.

Pashler, H., McDaniel, M., Rohrer, D., & Bjork, R. (2008). Learning styles: Concepts and evidence. *Psychological Science in the Public Interest*, 9(3), 105-119.

Petty, B. J. (2018). *Illuminate: Technology enhanced learning*. EdTechTeam Press.

Piaget, J. (1980). *To understand is to invent*. Penguin Books.

Pollard, A. (1997). *Reflective teaching in the primary school: A handbook for the classroom*. Cassell.

Priddis, L., & Rogers, S. L. (2018). Development of the reflective practice questionnaire: preliminary findings. *Reflective Practice, 19*(1), 89-104. https://doi.org/10.1080/14623943.2017.1379384

Rawlings, R. (2019, June 18). Mastering the protege effect: What decades of experience teaches us about learning. *Age of Awareness*. https://medium.com/age-of-awareness/mastering-the-protege-effect-1a49c62f7be5

Rhonda's contribution (journaling) [E-mail to the author]. (2019, July 8).

Ritchie, J. (n.d.). *What is an infographic. What they are and why they're useful*. Column Five. https://www.columnfivemedia.com/infographic

Rock, H. (2002). Job-embedded professional development and reflective coaching. *The Instructional Leader, 5*(8), 1-4.

Romero Grimaldo, L. (2020, Feb 6). *Literacy interventions for English learners* [Colloquium session]. Portland State University Research Colloquium, Portland, Oregon, United States.

Salva, C., & Matis, A. (2017). *Boosting achievement: Reaching students with interrupted or minimal education*. Seidlitz Education.

Samson, J. F., & Collins, B. A. (2012). *Preparing all teachers to meet the needs of English language learners: Applying research to policy and practice for teacher effectiveness*. Center for American Progress. https://eric.ed.gov/?id=ED535608

Schwartz, K. (2017, October 22). *How school leaders can attend to the emotional side of change*. KQED. https://www.kqed.org/mindshift/49486/how-school-leaders-can-attend-to-the-emotional-side-of-change

Seashore, K., Anderson, A., & Riedel, E. (2003). *Implementing arts for academic achievement: The impact of mental models, professional community and interdisciplinary teaming*. Center for Applied Research and Educational Improvement. https://hdl.handle.net/11299/143717

Seidlitz, J., & Perryman, B. (2011). *7 steps to a language-rich interactive classroom: Research-based strategies for engaging all students*. Seidlitz Education.

Shory, M., & McGarth, I. (2019, August 25). *Scaffolds for ELs* [pdf]. https://drive.google.com/file/d/124XTlzRAlotAm0rvbnIzP3zSiZ7_MKZ-/view

Slavin, R.E. (1991). Synthesis of research on cooperative learning. *Educational Leadership, 48*(5), 71-82.

Smiciklas, M. (2012). *The power of infographics: Using pictures to communicate and connect with your audiences*. Que Publishing.

Stoll, L., Bolam, R., McMahon, A., Wallace, M., & Thomas, S. (2006). Professional learning communities: A review of the literature. *Journal of Educational Change, 7*(4), 221-258. https://doi.org/10.1007/s10833-006-0001-8

Tang, E., & Lam, C. (2014). Building an effective online learning community (OLC) in blog-based teaching portfolios. *The Internet and Higher Education, 20*(1), 79-85. https://doi.org/10.1016/j.iheduc.2012.12.002

TESOL Writing Team. (2018). *The 6 principles for exemplary teaching of English learners: Grades K-12*. TESOL Press.

The Yale Center for Dyslexia & Creativity. (2014, Nov 7). *Evidence-based vs research based programs for dyslexics* [Video]. Youtube. https://www.youtube.com/watch?v=nbQ9wAtTxlU

Toppel, K. (2011, Jan 8). Tough. *Sneaker Teacher*. http://sneakerteacher.blogspot.com/2011/01/tough.html

Toppel, K. (2018, Nov 2). How every teacher can be a teacher of language. *Empowering ELLs*. https://www.empoweringells.com/teacheroflanguage/

Toppel, K.E. (2013). *The call for cultural responsiveness: Teachers' perceptions about the interplay between culturally responsive instruction and scripted curricula*. [Doctoral dissertation, Portland State University]. PDXScholar. https://doi.org/10.15760/etd.1002

Tschida, C. M., Ryan, C. L., & Ticknor, A. S. (2014). Building on windows and mirrors: Encouraging the disruption of "single stories" through children's literature. *Journal of Children's Literature, 40*(1), 28-39.

Valentina: Sketch note contribution [E-mail to T. K. Huynh]. (2019, September 21).

Vo, J. [@JennyVo15]. (2017, July 3). In just one day on Twitter, I've learned how to use snapchat, booksnap, bitmoji, and GIFs! [GIF attached] [Tweet]. Twitter. https://twitter.com/JennyVo15/status/882077803604258817

Wammes, J. D., Meade, M. E., & Fernandes, M. A. (2016). The drawing effect: Evidence for reliable and robust memory benefits in free recall. *The Quarterly Journal of Experimental Psychology*, 69, 1752-1776.

Wei, R. C., Darling-Hammond, L., Andree, A., Richardson, N., Orphanos, S. (2009). *Professional learning in the learning profession: A status report on teacher development in the United States and abroad.* National Staff Development Council.

Weinberger, D. (2014). *Too big to know: rethinking knowledge now that the facts aren't the facts, experts are everywhere, and the smartest person in the room is the room.* Basic Books.

Whitby, T. (2013, Nov 18). How do I get a PLN? *Edutopia.* https://www.edutopia.org/blog/how-do-i-get-a-pln-tom-whitby

WIDA. (2020). WIDA English language development standards framework, 2020 edition: Kindergarten-grade 12. Board of Regents of the University of Wisconsin System.

Williams, M. (1989). Vygotsky's social theory of mind. *Harvard Educational Review*, 59(1), 108-126. https://doi.org/10.17763/haer.59.1.t7002347m8710618

Winn, Ross. (2020, March 7). *2020 Podcast Stats & Facts* (New Research From Jan 2020). Podcast Insights®. Retrieved March 15, 2020, from www.podcastinsights.com/podcast-statistics/

Yang, K. (2019). *Front desk.* Scholastic Inc.

Yang, S. H. (2009). Using blogs to enhance critical reflection and community of practice. *Educational Technology & Society*, 12(2), 11-21.

Zacarian, D., & Silverstone, M. (2020). *Teaching to empower: Taking action to foster student agency, self-confidence, and collaboration.* ASCD.

Zwiers, J. (2019). *The communication effect: How to enhance learning by building ideas and bridging information gaps.* Corwin.

SEIDLITZ EDUCATION BOOK ORDER FORM

  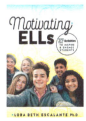 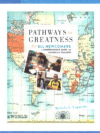  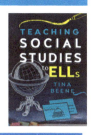

TITLE	PRICE	QTY	TOTAL$	TITLE	PRICE	QTY	TOTAL$
38 Great Academic Language Builders	$24.95			Motivating ELLs: 27 Activities to Inspire & Engage Students	$26.95		
7 Pasos para crear un aula interactiva y rica en lenguaje SPANISH	$29.95			Navigating the ELPS: Using the Standards to Improve Instruction for English Learners	$24.95		
7 Steps to a Language-Rich Interactive Classroom	$29.95			Navigating the ELPS: Math 2ND ED.	$29.95		
7 Steps To a Language-Rich, Interactive Foreign Language Classroom	$32.95			Navigating the ELPS: Science	$29.95		
				Navigating the ELPS: Social Studies	$29.95		
Boosting Achievement: Reaching Students with Interrupted or Minimal Education	$26.95			Navigating the ELPS: Language Arts and Reading	$34.95		
				Optimizando el desarrollo de la lectoescritura SPANISH	$39.95		
Content Review & Practice for the TX ESL 154	$39.95			Pathways to Greatness for ELL Newcomers: A Comprehensive Guide for Schools & Teachers	$32.95		
Content Review & Practice for the TX Bilingual 164	$39.95			Reading & Writing with English Learners	$29.95		
Content Review & Practice for the TX Spanish 190	$39.95			RTI for ELLs Fold-Out	$16.95		
Diverse Learner Flip Book	$26.95			Sheltered Instruction in Texas: Second Language Acquisition Methods for Teachers of ELs	$29.95		
DIY PD: A Guide to Self-Directed Learning for Teachers of Multilingual Learners NEW!	$29.95			Talk Read Talk Write: A Practical Routine for Learning in All Content Areas K-12 2ND ED.	$32.95		
ELLs in Texas: What Teachers Need to Know 2ND ED.	$34.95			Teaching Social Studies to ELLs	$24.95		
ELs in Texas: What School Leaders Need to Know 3RD ED.	$34.95			Teaching Science to English Learners	$24.95		
ELPS Flip Book	$19.95			¡Toma la Palabra! SPANISH	$32.95		
English/Spanish Linguistic and Academic Connections	$29.95			Vocabulary Now! 44 Strategies All Teachers Can Use	$29.95		
Mi Cuaderno de Dictado SPANISH	$7.95						
	COLUMN 1 TOTAL $				COLUMN 2 TOTAL $		

Pricing, specifications, and availability subject to change without notice.

SHIPPING 9% of order total, minimum $14.95
5-7 business days to ship. If needed sooner please call for rates.
TAX EXEMPT? please fax a copy of your certificate along with order.

COLUMN 1+2	$
DISCOUNT	$
SHIPPING	$
TAX	$
TOTAL	$

HOW TO ORDER

PHONE **(210) 315-7119** | ONLINE at **www.seidlitzeducation.com**
FAX completed form with payment info to **(949) 200-4384**

NAME _____

SHIPPING ADDRESS _____ CITY _____ STATE, ZIP _____

PHONE NUMBER _____ EMAIL ADDRESS _____

TO ORDER BY FAX to **(949) 200-4384** please complete credit card info **or** attach purchase order

☐ Visa ☐ MasterCard ☐ Discover ☐ AMEX

CARD # _____ EXPIRES mm/yyyy
SIGNATURE _____ CVV _____
3- or 4- digit code

☐ **Purchase Order attached**
please make P.O. out to Seidlitz Education

For information about Seidlitz Education products and professional development, please contact us at
(210) 315-7119 | **kathy@johnseidlitz.com**
56 Via Regalo, San Clemente, CA 92673
www.seidlitzeducation.com

Giving kids the gift of **academic language**.™

REV08303021

SEIDLITZ PRODUCT ORDER FORM

Three ways to order

- **FAX** completed order form with payment information to **(949) 200-4384**
- **PHONE** order information to **(210) 315-7119**
- **ORDER ONLINE** at **www.seidlitzeducation.com**

Pricing, specifications, and availability subject to change without notice.

TITLE	Price	QTY	TOTAL $
Instead Of I Don't Know Poster For the LOTE Classroom 24" x 36"	**3 pack**			
☐ LOTE FRENCH	$29.85		
☐ LOTE SPANISH	$29.85		
☐ LOTE GERMAN	$29.85		
☐ LOTE ARABIC **NEW!**	$29.85		
☐ LOTE CHINESE **NEW!**	$29.85		
	TOTAL $		

TITLE	Price	QTY	TOTAL $
Instead Of I Don't Know Poster, 24" x 36"	**3 pack**			
☐ Elementary ENGLISH	$29.85		
☐ Secondary ENGLISH	$29.85		
Instead Of I Don't Know Posters, 11" x 17"	**20 pack**			
☐ Elementary ENGLISH	$40.00		
☐ Secondary ENGLISH	$40.00		
Instead Of I Don't Know Poster, 24" x 36"	**3 pack**			
Elementary SPANISH	$29.85		
Instead Of I Don't Know Posters, 11" x 17"	**20 pack**			
Elementary SPANISH	$40.00		
	TOTAL $		

TITLE	Price	QTY	TOTAL $
Academic Language Cards and Activity Booklet, ENGLISH	$19.95		
Academic Language Cards, SPANISH	$9.95		
	TOTAL $		

TITLE	Price	QTY	TOTAL $
Please Speak In Complete Sentences Poster 24" x 36"	**3 pack**			
☐ ENGLISH ☐ SPANISH	$29.85		
Please Speak In Complete Sentences Posters, 11" x 17"	**20 pack**			
☐ ENGLISH ☐ SPANISH	$40.00		
	TOTAL $		

SHIPPING 9% of order total, minimum $14.95 5-7 business days to ship. If needed sooner please call for rates.

TAX EXEMPT? please fax a copy of your certificate along with order.

GRAND TOTAL	$
DISCOUNT	$
SHIPPING	$
TAX	$
FINAL TOTAL	$

NAME _____

SHIPPING ADDRESS _____ CITY _____ STATE, ZIP _____

PHONE NUMBER _____ EMAIL ADDRESS _____

TO ORDER BY FAX to **(949) 200-4384** please complete credit card info **or** attach purchase order

☐ Visa ☐ MasterCard ☐ Discover ☐ AMEX

CARD # _____ EXPIRES _____ mm/yyyy

SIGNATURE _____ CVV _____

☐ **Purchase Order**

please make P.O. out to Seidlitz Education